Praise

"This book covers big picture concepts, how companies who still rely on a single market are truly exposed to much higher risk. So, with the aid of this valuable book, look to exporting, licensing, franchising and joint ventures. Growing globally is no longer a luxury, it's a necessity".

Jane Malyon - Chief Scone Gnome
The English Cream Tea Company Ltd

"For nearly 30 years Levent has been consistently banging the drum to encourage companies, seeking to develop export markets, to have effective language strategies in place before they set off on that journey. Now they can stop wondering why their companies aren't performing better or making the breakthroughs they set their sights on. Good Business in any Language should find its way onto every exporter's desk, to be used as the 'go-to' reference guide".

Geoffrey Bowden - General Secretary
European Union of Associations of Translation Companies

"Levent has managed to identify the weaknesses in many organisations that see themselves as successful but could be far more profitable if they started to look at themselves through the eyes of other cultures".

John Brandler - Director & Founder
Thesam (Street Art Museum)

"Growing globally is a daunting challenge for any business – so many unknowns to grapple with! This book provides essential, practical guidance and useful tips for understanding international trading opportunities. Packed with sound advice it is a must-read for those wanting to develop a clear strategy and confidence to get their company ready for exporting".

Shireen Smith – Lawyer
Author of Brand Tuned, the new rules of branding, strategy and intellectual property

"To succeed globally, you must see your brand through the eyes of your stakeholders! Understanding what motivates your employees, investors, and customers, is vital. Levent's book acts as a practical guide to help to navigate the complex global world we now work in".

Domenica di Lieto – CEO
Emerging Communications–Anglo/Chinese Digital Marketing Consultancy

"Global growth requires a global mindset: how true! The LINGO model, detailing insights, tips and examples, will help SME leaders excel on a global stage. Levent's curiosity, passion and considerable experience shines through. It's a potent mix!"

Kevin Johnson – Group Chair and CEO Coach
Vistage International

"Good business in any language is an essential tool to understanding the global opportunities for businesses. Filled with very useful statistics, helpful tips, and eye-opening information, it is the essential guide to take your business to a global level or to develop your existing operation further.

Getting it right saves time, money, builds relationships and inspires confidence, leading to exponential growth".

Joel Van Der Molen
Vandercom Films

"Good Business In Any Language an easy to follow, comprehensive look at global trade for entrepreneurs and business owners.

It contains a step by step guide to taking your business global. Each has astute takeaways, which I especially liked. The book truly shows the importance of effective communication when overcoming language and cultural barriers and how this can translate to global growth".

Zeynep Turudi – MD
Truede Ltd, D.I.T Export Champion

"This book should be in every DIT ITA's briefcase, when first discussing exporting with a client. I would like to see this book as the 'go to' reference for future business owners, export managers and their teams. Levent's knowledge and skills need to be used to form a part of a company's total exporting ethos".

Stuart Gibbons OBE - MD
Le Mark Group, D.I.T Export Champion

"People who are interested in internationalisation should take stock from Levent's reflections and the LINGO model. Gaining new prospective on global markets, approaching them with a fresh new angle is thought and action provoking: 5 easy steps in a 5 star book".

Giovanni Baccini - Managing Director
Lewden

"As always, Levent offers sensible and relevant advice in this book. In our long experience with cross language communication, having seen companies make the same expensive mistakes and ineffective choices. Make this your essential reading if you are trading internationally".

Susannah Poulton - International Trade Adviser

"Whether you thinking about or already trading in the global market, read this book! Understanding the motivation of your investors, employees, stakeholders, and customers from varying geographical markets is crucial to success in the international market. This book is a practical, no-nonsense guide that will undoubtedly crack the "going-global" nutshell with success".

Maggie Gilbert - Marketing Professional

"The best opportunity to scale business is to trade globally, however getting it right typically takes decades of experience. To avoid the pitfalls when expanding internationally, take advantage of Levent's experience and read Good Business in Any Language".

Stephen Bavister - Author & Business Growth Consultant

Speak the lingo of global business

Good Business in any Language

HOW TO THRIVE IN GLOBAL MARKETS

LEVENT YILDIZGOREN

Drawings by Janet Nerding

Typesetting by Denise Robinson
www.ttcwetranslate.com

Dedication

I dedicate this to my family who have been my strength, support and sounding board throughout the years and particularly to my late father who has always made all his resources available for mine and my sister's education. It would have been a great pleasure for me to share my book with him.

Contents

Introduction

I've never understood why smart executives spend thousands of pounds going on a trade mission to a foreign country without doing even basic preparation. Something as simple as having business cards in the local language has a huge impact on the success of their mission. It may be the difference between opening the door to global trade for their business and finding it's securely locked.

It's not unusual to find cases where basic market research would have saved money – and sometimes, embarrassment too.

I realised that these oversights weren't due to trying to shortcut the process or save money, but simply because the business didn't have any kind of blueprint to follow. It's not a problem only experienced by smaller companies – companies of all sizes have made the same mistakes. The businesses that have successfully gone global are the ones that have a structured plan to follow.

- Many medium-sized UK businesses shy away from selling to global markets thinking that this is only something big businesses can do successfully
- Some businesses try to replicate their UK activities in other countries, thinking that what works in the UK will work elsewhere

- Many SMEs resist going global due to fear of the unknown. Languages and culture appear to be the biggest factors that contribute to this. After all, language is what enables us to communicate our wants and needs and understand those of others and culture is understanding how things are done in a particular environment.

Then there are the short-term challenges that have been created by post-Brexit regulations and restrictions imposed due to the COVID-19 pandemic.

Many UK businesses who are engaged in trade with any of the EU countries are finding it hard to adapt to new regulations.

In January 2021 UK exports to EU countries were reduced almost by half.

This new situation makes growing your businesses overseas harder. You must do all of these things, while trying to grow your business and control the costs.

In addition to the post-Brexit challenges your business may be affected by the restrictions imposed due to the global pandemic. This has also put some industries, such as automotive, under pressure.

In the long-term, the increasing competition from other countries, such as the increase of the Chinese manufacturing industry, may give you concerns. To continue growing, you must increase your market share and expand to new countries.

It's important that you find solutions quickly to overcome the current challenges. If you don't take action your company's growth may come to a halt. Increasing customer engagement in global markets is crucial to prevent revenues reducing.

I have noticed even experienced executives are making mistakes that are, essentially, preventing them from reaching their full potential globally.

If you feel you've hit the limit of your local market, competition has reduced your market share, or you're frustrated with the growth in your domestic market, then expanding to global markets is an ideal solution.

The secret of success is to have a framework to work within.

Is this book for you?

If you are in the process of expanding into a new export market, or if you are a business owner wondering why your investment is not working as well as you expected, this book will give you a solid foundation to research, prepare and implement a global strategy.

Instead of waiting to come across challenges you'll explore strategies to avoid the usual pitfalls so you can:

- Identify which product or service is best suited to your target customers
- Prevent product recalls
- Form better relations with your partners or distributors in these countries.

During my 30 years working with dozens of UK and international companies, I've gained invaluable experience in localisation and the impact it has on global sales. I have a passion for helping companies to grow internationally.

I don't pretend to have all the answers, and we have made our own mistakes. Our attempt to grow our business in Germany was not successful; it cost us money and time. However, I learned a lot from the first-hand experience, and now I want to pass on these useful lessons to you!

That's why I have put together the simple, 5-step LINGO model.

This book is for you, if:
- You are already selling globally, but not getting high returns on your investment
- You are looking to expand to new export markets, but not sure which one to choose
- You have never traded globally but would like to get started.

How to use this book

This book will help you to focus on the fundamentals of running a thriving global business. Whether your business provides services or goods, the 5-step LINGO model will give you a framework so you don't miss any essential steps in your global journey.

In Part one, you will find details of the current situation and opportunities growing globally provides and shows how UK SMEs are currently positioned in this regard.

Part two is about going global. It outlines the basic principles of how to reach international customers and different routes of access.

Part three is the implementation process. It will provide you with tools to choose a new export market, how to assess it and how to roll out your sales strategy.

The LINGO model is the foundation that underpins successful global trading:

- **L**earn the market
- **I**nformation gathering
- **N**avigate the market
- **G**o operational
- **O**pen for business

I encourage you to go through each step. Some of the steps will resonate more with you depending on where you are in your global journey.

The LINGO model will help you to set up a structure to thrive in a global market and repeat the same process for any new export market you intend to expand into.

There are case studies and quick tips to help you to avoid the pitfalls, to share best practice and provide a robust route to a successful global growth.

Time to start your journey of discovery!

Part One: The Current Situation and Global Opportunities

The world has changed drastically since March 2020. What we accepted as normal regarding buying, selling and travelling for personal or business is no longer simple.

The volatility the pandemic has brought to our lives has created even more interesting times for business. We have seen some businesses flourish; others experience hard times and some that have managed to pivot and continued to grow.

Like any crisis, it has brought threats and opportunities at the same time.

While some countries are struggling to overcome the effect of the pandemic, a few countries have managed to find ways to prosper. For instance, China's economy grew 18.3% in the first quarter of 2021.

The global pandemic has shown that the companies who rely on a single market are exposed to higher risk when there are unexpected changes. Companies who operate in multiple markets are more flexible and able to contain any crisis they may face and more likely to continue with their usual business.

However, going global is a big step to take and it's easy to make mistakes such as:

- Trying to replicate what worked in the domestic market
- Not planning the process from top down

- Not doing enough market research
- Not following a structure or a model for growing globally
- Not taking into account the buying behaviours of the target market.

I have developed the simple, 5-step LINGO model as a result of working with dozens of companies over the last three decades. The step-by-step guide ensures you don't miss any of the crucial steps. Among other things, you will discover the critical data and information to ensure that the new export market is a suitable one for your business.

The 5-step LINGO model is based on the following principles:

Step 1: Learn the market

This is the research step. This is where you research new export markets that are suitable for your product or service before taking any steps. Only after the completion of this step is it advisable to move forward. This stage ensures there is potential for the company's product or service and that the target market has a suitable economic structure.

In this stage you will discover if there is a sufficient volume of demand for your products or services, and if it makes financial sense for you to invest there.

Step 2: Information gathering

This is the analysis step. When you have chosen a new export market it's time to analyse the market in more depth to make sure you can roll out your products or services successfully. This step is essential for assessing market potential and finding out all market specific requirements such as distribution, packaging labelling and competition for calculating your return on investment.

This step will ensure that you are fully aware if your products or services need any modifications or if there are any special labelling requirements. This has everything to do with finding your way in the new market, so that you can calculate the true cost of deploying the product or service to the new country, making sure there are no surprise costs.

Step 3: Navigate the market

This is pre-implementation step. Now that you are satisfied about new market's potential it's time to start planning. If you export products, this includes finding local distributors and arranging storage facilities. If you export services, finding out about local VAT regulations and joint venture partners. In both cases making deals and negotiations, all critical before full deployment.

This step is about getting strategic information together and preparing for the roll out. You can do most of the research from your desk. You could also join a trade mission to the country to get on the ground information and a feel for the country yourself. It is worth exploring potential joint venture opportunities with non-competing companies that have similar target audiences.

Any of these activities will help you to understand how business is done in the country and help you to discover how best to reach and engage your new market.

You may need to explore alternative methods of information gathering if there are travel restrictions due to the pandemic or any other circumstances that make travelling to the country inadvisable.

Step 4: Go operational

This is the implementation step where the previous three steps will come together. Companies who cannot get to this stage in a timely manner can end up wasting resources or, in the best-case scenario, losing market share to their competitors, as time to market entry can be critical for some products or services.

It's essential that you understand the market and use the checklists I refer to in chapter 9 to make sure you are ready to start with the implementation process.

Once this step is in place, then you need to consider keeping up-to-date with changing trends and legal requirements as well as mitigating unforeseen circumstances.

Step 5: Open for business

This is the running and monitoring step. Now operations are ongoing, progress is being monitored, any minor obstacles along the way should be easily resolved at this stage. You are no longer looking at this as a new possibility, but a new market where you are fully operational and ready to expand further.

If you are feeling overwhelmed with the current situation or are limited in your domestic market, the next three chapters will explore the benefits of globalisation.

In these chapters we will look at why international trade is no longer 'nice-to-have' but a necessity and we'll explore globalisation issues. We'll take a look at the benefits of doing business internationally and the cost of reluctance to take action.

Chapter 1 Why Go Global?

International trade is nothing new, trading between countries and across the continents has always taken place. The Silk Road was a historic trade route from 2nd Century B.C. until the 18th Century A.D. connecting East to West. It was central to economic, cultural, religious, and political interactions as news, influences and, of course, money was passed between traders.

Countries generally engaged in international trade to get the products and materials they lacked in exchange for the products they produced in abundance. Today, international trade is embedded in almost every industry. Children's toys, clothes, electronic goods, and food all feature in international trade agreements.

International trade also includes service industries. While services such as banking, communications, financial services are intangible, they still have value internationally. In developed economies the service sector has grown steadily over the years. In the USA the service sector accounted for more than half of the gross domestic product in 1929 and by 1993 it accounted for more than two thirds. Today, the service sector accounts for 60% of the global GDP and employs more than 60% of the labour force worldwide.

Therefore, international trade has a valuable place in relation to the development and growth of most SMEs.

International trade, sometimes referred to as cross-border trading or global trading, has many benefits. If you are not already doing so, I hope you'll find the information I'm sharing will encourage you to get started.

If you are already selling internationally, it will encourage you to continue with your journey and may provide you with additional tips to help you thrive globally.

How it all started

Back in the 15th-16th centuries most countries in Europe based their economic policy on maximising exports while minimising imports into the country by introducing high tariffs and import duties. This was known as Mercantilism and functioned as one nation could only increase its wealth at the expense of others. The policy was simple; encouraged exports, minimised imports and the surplus was invested in gold. As you can imagine, this policy often led to conflicts and wars. By the 19th century the mercantilist laws and policies started to disappear.

Free trade for all

Economists based in France and England started to reject mercantilism by the middle of 18th century. They believed that there had to be a fairer way to trade.

Most notably in England, Adam Smith in his book The Wealth of Nations (1776) defended the advantages of trading without restrictions. In France, the group of economists known as Physiocrats demanded freedom of production and trade. As a result, the Anglo–French Treaty of 1786 was signed, ending the trade war between two countries. Then in 1860, the Anglo–French trade agreement was a clear win for liberal ideas, reducing French import duties to a maximum of 25% within 5 years and free entry of French products into Britain. Many other trade agreements followed soon after between other countries.

Then it all came apart

World Wars I and II brought havoc to trade agreements and practically introduced a new version of mercantilism. The Great Depression in 1930 meant that countries attempted to shore up their finances as unemployment reached epidemic levels. As a result, protectionist measures were introduced resulting in import quotas with some countries banning imports altogether.

After the end of World War II, trade agreements became the main method of managing and promoting international trade.

What is globalisation?

Globalisation is described as the process of interaction and integration between people, companies, and governments worldwide (Wikipedia). It has been made much easier due to technological advances in communication and transportation.

There are many positive aspects of globalisation as well as some negatives. In underdeveloped countries globalisation is perceived to play a negative role, even though it brings jobs and security to these areas.

There are parts of globalisation that are said to kill innovation and development of local businesses. For example, restaurants, small corner shops and local supermarkets can lose out to big chains; multinational companies can dominate in any country.

Large companies use the global economy to their advantage. IBM gets over 60% of sales outside the USA, runs its human resources from Manila, accounting from Kuala Lumpur, procurement from Shenzhen and customer service from Brisbane for its Japanese business.

The global economy is interconnected and what happens in one part of the world inevitably affects other parts. My point of view is based on how it impacts on the global growth of SMEs.

In today's global economy, most large companies no longer limit their activities to their local markets. They set up production and sales centres around the globe, covering different time zones. This has changed the way we do business in the 21st century. Medium-sized companies cannot afford to ignore the global economy as a force to be reckoned with in every aspect of industry and sales.

Smaller countries have more incentive to be part of the global economy, because the smaller the country, the smaller and more limited its domestic market is. By being part of the global economy, they can benefit from countries with large-scale production capabilities. Even a large country, such as the USA, gains a lot by exporting to other countries and benefits from their often lower-cost production capabilities.

This has made the largest companies fully dependent on the global economy to maximise their returns, like their supply chains and production, as well as their global customers. Without the global economy, they would not have a fraction of their wealth.

A new perspective

Today, international trade has taken on a new dimension and no country can afford to be isolated from it. Countries' economies somehow depend on each other and that makes international trade and cooperation even more important.

For your business to prosper you should embrace international trade into your business culture and operations. A medium-sized company without this perspective is likely to hit a barrier at some stage in their progress. When the company starts seeing lower returns from their domestic market or the market gets saturated and does not offer any growth opportunities, it's time to look further afield.

Executives who embrace international trade into their company culture have new options to explore. A small company employing up to 10 people with a turnover of, say, £1 million, can make product adaptations and new market decisions a lot quicker than bigger organisations.

Often the owner or majority shareholder of the company is the main decision maker, and they can roll out to a new country market a lot quicker than a medium-sized company employing 100 people with a comprehensive product and a more complex decision making structure. Therefore, embracing international trade culture is even more critical for medium-sized companies.

The benefits of Going Global

Companies who trade internationally are more likely to survive than the ones who do not and international trade fuels innovation and creativity. As a result, companies and their staff develop and have a different dynamic, working to their advantage.

Trading globally provides many benefits:

Reduced dependence on your local market

Your home market may be struggling due to economic pressures, but if you go global, you will have immediate access to a practically unlimited range of customers in areas where there is more money available to spend. Because different cultures have different wants and needs, you can diversify your product range to take advantage of these differences.

Increased chances of success

Unless you have got your pricing wrong, the higher the volume of products you sell, the more profit you make, and overseas trade is an obvious way to increase sales. In support of this, UK Trade and Investment (UKTI) claim that companies who go global are 12% more likely to survive and excel than those that choose not to export.

Increased efficiency

Go global and profitably use up any excess capacity in your business. This leverages economies of scale and smooths out production schedules, avoiding the seasonal peaks and troughs that are the bane of the production manager's life.

Better risk management

When you export products or services you get the full benefit of diversification. When you operate only in your domestic market, you will have an increased risk from any economic downturns, political factors, environmental events. You can mitigate potential risks much easier when you are less dependent on a single market.

Economic advantage

Take advantage of currency fluctuations – export when the value of the pound sterling is low against other currencies and reap the very real benefits. Words of warning though; watch out for import tariffs in the country you are exporting to and keep an eye on the value of sterling. You do not want to be caught out by any sudden upsurge in the value of the pound, or you could lose all the profit you have worked so hard to gain.

Innovation

Because you are exporting to a wider range of customers, you will also gain a wider range of feedback about your products, and this can lead to real benefits. In fact, UKTI statistics show that businesses believe exporting leads to innovation and increases in break-through product development to solve problems and meet the needs of the wider customer base. 53% of businesses they spoke to said that a new product or service has evolved because of the demands of international trade.

Growth

The holy grail for any business is growth, and this is something that has been lacking in the UK's manufacturing industry. International trade generally creates increased growth. And the growth of your company benefits both your business and the country's economy.

Multiply your business

Companies who struggle to grow in their domestic markets may possibly have an opportunity in other countries. Pretty much all countries are part of the global economy and this makes it likely that another country may need your products or services and there may not even be strong competition. This presents an opportunity to grow and even double your business.

If your company already has a global presence, it is possible to look for additional countries to add to those you are already trading with. And again, the tips and tools offered here will be useful for you. After all, you have already seen the benefits of trading globally and it makes perfect sense to increase your reach and fuel your growth further.

I suggest that you try a variety of ways to determine new or additional markets and not rely on just one type of activity or hearsay or somebody else's experience. Because what may work for one company may not be suitable for you. However, it is also true that it could be the other way round – another company's failure in a country could be exactly the right fit for your company – providing you carry out thorough research.

Top 10 Internet languages – March 2021

Language	Number of Internet Users
English	1,186,451,052
Chinese	888,453,068
Spanish	363,684,593
Arabic	237,418,349
Indonesian/Malaysian	198,029,815
Portuguese	171,750,818
French	151,733,611
Japanese	118,626,672
Russian	116,353,942
German	92,525,427
Total	3,525,027,347

Source: https://www.internetworldstats.com/stats7.htm

It is interesting that the top 10 languages cover 76.9% of the world's internet population according to 31 March 2021 Internet World Stats. English on its own only covers 25.9% of the internet population according to the same data. This means if your website or marketing brochures are in English only, your reach to global audiences will be limited. And by making information available in the top ten languages, you have the potential of reaching nearly 77% of the internet population.

Another interesting fact is that internet users' penetration rate in India is 5.8% which is much lower than English speaking countries or China. This presents a massive future opportunity if you have an e-commerce business, as India has a large population still not using online services. In China. 60.1% of the population use the Internet and this reflects in their e-commerce volumes.

Valentine's Day vs Singles Day

Valentine's Day is celebrated every year on 14 February. It's the day when people show affection for another person by sending cards, gifts or flowers with messages of love. This is an important day for retail. Americans spent $27.4 billion and UK shoppers spent nearly £1 billion in 2020. China, however, has Singles Day, which was originally called Bachelor's Day, celebrated on 11 November every year since 1993. On this day single people buy presents for themselves to celebrate being single.

The date 11 November (11/11) was chosen because 1 resembles a bare stick which is Chinese internet slang for unmarried man. This unofficial holiday in China has become the largest retail and online shopping day in the world. Chinese Alibaba and JD Retail China alone have grossed a record of $115 billion in sales across their platforms during the 2020 event. The record sales doubled from the previous year.

If you are an ecommerce executive this day can make a huge impact on your revenues. It is a known fact that British goods are respected and sought after by sophisticated Chinese consumers. This presents you with lucrative sales opportunities and this date needs to be in your calendar.

But the biggest question is how to reach out to the Chinese consumers and make that emotional connection that will lead them to buy your products (or services if you are in the service sector). What are the best channels and payment gateways that will enable you to achieve record sales in this sales bonanza? Hopefully, the LINGO process will help you to create and implement such a strategy.

Internet users worldwide

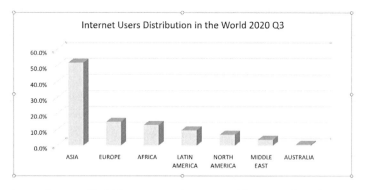

Source: *Internet World Stats – www.internetworldstats.com/stats.htm*

Basis: *4,929,926,187 Internet users in Sept 30 2020*

The above chart shows how internet users are distributed across the world. More than half of the users are based in Asia. Looking at this chart, can you visualise where your potential customers are based and are you able to reach them with your messages and information? What is the cost of missing a potential opportunity this size for your business?

Top countries for ease of doing business

The World Bank produces Doing Business reports every year detailing ease of doing business in each country. Every country from Afghanistan to Zimbabwe is included. The rankings are very detailed and cover everything from setting up business to resolving disputes and even ease of connecting utilities. This provides a wealth of information for executives for their decision making process.

Top 5 takeaways

1. Any size business can do international trade
2. Both product and service businesses can trade internationally
3. Trading internationally can benefit your business efficiency, innovation and reduce your risks
4. There is already data available that will help you make informed decisions about new export markets
5. International trade volume is consistently growing.

Summary

The figures show that global trade is increasing regardless of any crisis. For countries of all sizes, promoting international trade is the only way of to maintain prosperity.

On the other hand, international trade is no longer a luxury, but very much a necessity for growth and healthy development of most companies. The benefits of international trade outweigh any disadvantages by far.

It is also critical for executives of medium-sized companies to embrace the international trade culture so they don't miss the opportunities and benefits it can provide.

Chapter 2 Global Trade and the UK Scene

Global trade volume is increasing due to the opportunities created by collaboration and advancement in technology, including communication, delivery and transport facilities and advancement of payment gateways.

It's time to explore how the UK's small and medium-sized businesses are placed regarding global trade and the role trading globally can play in their growth.

Who is involved in the UK's global trade?

According to various surveys and research carried out by governments and other organisations, only 8% of the UK SMEs are involved in international trade. This rate is higher in most European countries, Germany being on top of the list. The UK is one of the bottom 5 countries in Europe in terms of export involvement by its SMEs according to the Centre for Economics and Business Research (CEBR) consultancy.

According to the Department for Business, Energy and Industrial Strategy, at the start of 2017:

- There were an estimated 5.7 million UK private sector businesses
- Only 1.3 million of these had employees

Even though there were only 7,285 large companies, they employed almost 40% of the UK workforce.

The table below shows this in detail:

	Businesses	Employment (thousands)	Turnover £ millions
All businesses	5,694,515	26,723	3,739,171
Sole traders & partnerships	4,327,680	4,697	271,574
1–9 employees	1,117,810	4,093	552,637
10–49 employees	207,885	4,059	539,786
50–249 employees	33,855	3,297	540,915
250 or more employees	7,285	10,577	1,834,259

Source: Department for Business, Energy and Industrial Strategy

https://www.gov.uk/government/statistics/business-population-estimates-2017

According to data published by the Department for Business and Innovation Skills on May 2016, only 9% of small and micro (0-49 employees) and 33% of medium (50-249 employees) firms export.

It seems that the UK's main export activity is carried out by large businesses. According to the Annual Business Survey (ABS) data, 43% of large businesses export. However only 33% of medium-sized businesses are involved in exporting. Increasing this percentage to around 45-50% would make a huge impact on the UK's economy.

UK's top 10 trading partners (2019)

Now let's have a look at the UK's top trading countries. These will provide some insights on to what to do next for executives new to international trade or the ones already doing it. It is important to take into account new trade deals that take place now or in the future. Also, it is possible that EU countries may not be the best matches for certain industries following the UK's exit from the EU.

Country	Total trade £bn	UK exports £bn	UK imports £bn
USA	229.9	140.9	89.0
Germany	132.7	55.1	77.6
Netherlands	92.0	40.9	51.1
China	86.1	36.7	49.5
France	85.4	40.7	44.7
Ireland	65.7	36.8	28.9

Country	Total trade £bn	UK exports £bn	UK imports £bn
Spain	50.3	18.7	31.6
Belgium	46.9	17.9	29.0
Italy	44.6	19.3	25.3
Switzerland	37.1	22.9	14.2

Source: ONS UK Trade, July to September 2020

The table above shows that 8 out of 10 top trading partners are from the EU countries. Something tells me that this table may not look the same by 2022.

If your business's main markets are based in the EU, then it may be to your benefit to re-calculate your return on investment.

If you are just starting to roll out to one of the EU countries, then it is important for you to thoroughly research details of the current trade deal in detail.

UK's total trade in goods and services

Now let's have a look at how products exports and service exports look regarding to total amount and what part they play.

	2019 £bn	2020 £bn
Goods	373.0	311.5
Services	316.3	260.2

Source: ONS UK Trade, July to September 2020

The table on the previous page shows over 25% reduction between 2019 and 2020 in both services and products exports. This is probably down to the effect of Brexit. When we think of exports generally, we may think of products. However, service exports are significantly close to the product exports.

UK's top 5 services exported (2019)

	£bn	% of total services exported
*Other business services	104.8	33.1
Financial Services	60.8	19.2
Travel Services	41.3	13.1
Transport Services	30.0	9.5
Telecoms, Computer and Information	22.2	7.0

*including professional, management consulting, technical and trade – related services

Source: ONS UK Trade, July to September 2020

UK's top 5 goods exports (2020)

	£bn	% of total goods exported
Cars	21.6	7.0
Medicine and Pharmaceutical Products	21.1	6.8
Mechanical Power Generators	20.5	6.6
Crude Oil	16.4	5.3
Non-Ferrous Metals	14.8	4.8

Source: ONS UK Trade, December 2020

The tables on the previous page present us with details of the top 5 products and services exports. It is striking that the top 5 goods industries only make up 30.5% of the total goods exported, whereas it is a different picture for the service exports.

The top 4 industries alone make up 48.8% of the total service industry.

How are the UK's SMEs positioned in global trade?

Lack of SMEs' involvement in international trade is creating a big gap in the UK's export capability. According to an article published in the Guardian, the UK is missing billions of pounds of export income.

According to a survey carried out by the Centre for Economics and Research Consultancy (CEBR) with bosses of 1,054 small and medium-sized companies, only 5% had plans to start exporting in the next five years.

It seems that if you are a medium-sized business executive, expanding into a new export market may not be your top priority for growth.

It is the book's aim to change this perception by providing a structure based on 5 simple steps to expand and thrive in global markets.

The micro and small company's perspective

In the UK, a micro company is defined as a business employing less than 10 employees and turnover less than £632,000 and a small company is defined as a business with a turnover of not more than £10.2 million and employs less than 50 employees.

It seems small and micro-sized companies are least likely to be trading globally. This is often due to their perceived knowledge about global trade and resources.

It is very easy to come up with 10 reasons not to do it. I believe it is very possible for small and micro businesses to trade globally - even from day one.

Once the process is put in place, it is often seen as a saviour that has arisen from the difficulties of challenging economic times.

I will share case studies throughout the book where the international trading has made a huge difference for a small business. And what better example than our own experiences.

Case study - TTC wetranslate Ltd, our own company

During the recession between 2008 and 2010 we were already trading globally with 30% of our company's revenue generated from our international customers. During that time many businesses in the UK had experienced drops in their revenues, including our business. As we were not relying on our domestic market alone, we were able to go through this period much easier.

During this recession, sterling lost around 25% of its value against the major currencies. For any business using international providers this was a disaster as it is not viable to absorb such a big drop.

Having international customers meant that we continued to receive payments in Euros and USDs which was a great help. Because of the payments we had received in Euros and USDs our exposure to currency fluctuations were limited.

This was a great opportunity to demonstrate that revenues coming globally provided the stability needed to run our businesses.

A medium-sized company's perspective

The term 'medium-sized company' covers a wide range of businesses. For our purposes the companies we are referring to as medium-sized employ fewer than 250 employees and have a turnover not more than £36 million.

In 2018, large businesses exported £70.5 billion, medium-sized businesses exported £34.8 billion and small businesses exported £25.6 billion. Considering the number of medium-sized businesses total 5 times more than large businesses, it is fair to say that most medium-sized businesses do not export.

What is holding back the medium-sized companies from trading globally? The answer to this has the potential to make a major impact on the UK's economy. This applies to the goods sector as well as the service sector. In recent years, we have seen many great examples of service sector companies achieving incredible growth. Below are couple of examples:

Streetbees, an AI driven human intelligence platform that collects and analyses offline consumer behaviour, founded in 2015 in London, now employs over 100 people and raised £30.7 million in October 2020 in Series B funding. Their turnover was £7 million on 30 August 2020.

> *Ventrica, based in Essex, help brands build stronger customer relationships and they also provide multilingual call centre services, employing over 250 people. Incorporated in 2009, company's turnover was £14 million at the October 2019.*

There are 33,855 medium size companies registered in the UK according to 2017 records. Currently only 33% of these are exporting.

Even a 5% increase would make a tangible difference in the UK economy.

The large company's perspective

A large company employs more than 250 employees and has a turnover over £36 million.

Most of the large businesses seem to be trading globally, with activities spanning many countries.

Even though there are far fewer they have higher turnovers nationally as well as internationally.

There are lessons to be learned from these large businesses as they consider global trade to be part of their strategy, integrating into how they operate.

Here are some examples:

Fitflop Ltd, *an iconic UK footwear brand known globally for their fashionable flip flops and sandals, had a turnover of $139 million in 2019, only 26% was from UK sales. The company was founded in November 2007 by Marcia Kilgore and had a global vision from their inception. By 31 December 2008, their UK sales were $10.7 million as opposed global sales of $27.9 million. This demonstrates what is possible once a brand targets going global.*

Teledyne UK Limited *(formerly e2v created by Marconi Electronics management buyout) develops and manufactures systems and components for space, life sciences and defence industries. Their export revenues are remarkably higher than their UK revenue. In 2019, almost 85% of their revenue came from global sales. As a result of their success, e2v were acquired by US company Teledyne Technologies in 2017.*

Another example of a large company with a significant global revenue is British video game developer **Jagex Limited.** *Founded in 1999 Jagex's turnover was £110 million at the end of December 2019, employing over 300 people in their Cambridge base. Due to its success, Jagex was acquired in 2012 by US investors and is currently owned by another US private equity company The Carlyle Group.*

There are many other examples of large companies achieving similar results.

The island challenge

The UK is an island nation surrounded by water and it is disconnected from the rest of the Europe. It is inevitable that there will be elements of the island mentality.

However, this should not pose a barrier in the age of fast communications and developed delivery networks.

Be aware of this disadvantage when looking for growth. It is a known fact that the countries with a common border are more likely to trade with each other.

Half of the UK's exports in 2019 were to EU countries. The USA trade more with Mexico and Canada than the rest of the world. The same thing happens between Scandinavian countries.

UK trade figures prove this point too. However, being disconnected physically may prevent UK business executives feeling that they are part of the European network, compared to European neighbouring countries. Being members of the EU means that these countries do not even have border controls between them, enabling the European economic network to work smoothly and easily.

Now the UK has left the EU, there is not only a physical barrier, but also the added challenge of export and import duties and paperwork. However, it's worthwhile remembering the advantage of trading with neighbouring countries. Fortunately, there are trade agreements with the EU covering most industries, which means close to 'business as usual' for the majority of UK companies.

Brexit, the EU and global trade

The UK's exit from the EU will have a lasting effect on the UK's economy and, for better or for worse, will shape the UK's global trade, including relations with EU countries.

Currently half of the UK's exports go to EU countries. For some companies their exports to the EU constitute the majority of their export activity. Naturally, these company executives are among the most concerned about the adverse effects of Brexit.

A change of circumstances requires a changed approach and mindset. Smart CEOs and CFOs will follow political developments carefully.

However, the biggest benefit will come from using this as an opportunity to review global strategy and product development and help to bring a major shift in your company's global approach. There is the potential to extend your company's reach to new territories.

The post-Brexit impact is still not fully known at the time of writing. There may be some glitches over the years and it is best that you are prepared for this.

A good example of this is the row that took place in May 2021 between London and France about the post-Brexit fishing rights.

France threatened to cut off Jersey's electricity if there was no agreement about the fishing rights between the countries. Luckily no drastic action was taken by either country.

The SMEs view of political developments

Should SMEs take political developments into account? As some of the political developments are likely to effect the trade relations, the answer should be 'Yes'. Also, executives should be aware of any regional conflicts.

This is an important factor, particularly for large companies. For example, a UK company, Vodaphone, has many times more subscribers in India than they have in the UK.

They employ thousands of employees in India. Any new legislation with the country as well as any changes in the international law will have a direct impact on their business.

Some British brands, such as Mothercare (now operating overseas only) and Marks and Spencer's, have branches in many countries around the globe and have an exposure to international developments.

As a company executive you can only consider the existing conditions (unless you have a crystal ball to see into the future). That doesn't mean you should stop considering global trade, but you should include contingency plans in your overall strategy. You can gather valuable information by observing the current political climate from the many available channels without becoming a political analyst.

A few years ago political changes in Cuba resulted in the lifting of some sanctions. This has provided an opportunity of a new holiday destination for tour operators. So, political developments can have both negative and positive effects.

There could be adverse effects too. A confectionary manufacturer lost an export market because their products originated from a country that is in conflict with the country they are exporting to.

Their customer in the export market will not accept products originated from the country they are in conflict with.

There will always be events outside your control that unfold during your company's global journey. However, the whole essence of the 'going global' mindset will minimise these unforeseen factors as you will always be aware of the developments taking place where you are trading, as well as continuing to look for new potential markets.

It is critical that executives do their due diligence regardless of their size. This could be less critical for e-commerce companies, where the goods are marketed and sold via their websites and they will be less affected than those who are on the ground. Nevertheless, due diligence can save time and effort for all types of businesses.

Top 5 takeaways

1. In the UK most large companies are involved in international trade

2. British goods and services are respected internationally

3. Small and micro-sized businesses are least involved in international trade

4. Medium-sized companies are missing out on growth due to not trading internationally and even a small increase would impact the UK's economy for the better

5. To prevent any surprises, it is important that you follow political developments in your export markets.

Summary

While most UK companies involved in international trade are large organisations, there is a huge potential for medium-sized and even small businesses to get involved in export activities. The right mindset is important for success in going global.

A global market reduces the impact of local influences and helps your company to maintain growth and profitability.

Chapter 3 Excuses, excuses!

Many obstacles prevent companies from growth. These can be technical, financial, logistical or staff difficulties. However, one of the most common difficulties facing SMEs is executives' reluctance to take action.

There are situations where an executive has done the planning, carried out market research and is almost ready to roll out, but they simply cannot make the final decision.

This 'wait and see' approach may be avoiding risk, but it can easily kill the momentum and, in some cases, can even leave the market open for competition to move in.

Due diligence and planning are essential for succeeding in a new export market. However, it is equally important to take timely action to make it happen.

You can overcome the fear of the unknown by doing comprehensive due diligence. Following a structured model, such as the LINGO model, will guide you in this journey so you are confident that you've explored all the angles and have solid information to work on. No excuses for not proceeding!

How globalisation is shaping trade & e-commerce

When it comes to certain trades it is not possible to think other than in global terms. But it was not like this 10 years ago. Most of the things we buy, sell or produce involve global trade or a part or component comes from a global trade activity. The headphones I have are produced in China, but designed by a British company. It could be a garment bought from a Spanish company (e.g. Mango or Zara) designed in Italy, conceptualised in Spain, with buttons from Poland and produced in India. Most of things we buy and use are created as a result of global trade.

Globalisation is shaping trade in many ways. One point of view is that it is rapidly filling any gaps in the market that are profitable, not allowing small local businesses to thrive. Existing businesses can find it hard to compete with experienced global organisations. If you imagine a sandwich shop serving customers during late morning and lunch time. Then along comes a company like Subway offering similar products, employing students, working as many hours as they can get permission from local authorities. This makes it very hard for a small business owner to compete with a global brand that has a vast number of resources.

Globalisation has fundamentally changed e-commerce. The concept of drop-shipping was not even heard of until a few years ago. Now anyone can sell any item without holding any stock, due to advancements in logistics systems and payment gateways.

There are so many e-commerce platforms that facilitate selling globally and without many costs or setting up time. The best known ones are eBay, Alibaba and Etsy, but there are many others.

Don't overlook payment processes

Chinese e-commerce is much more advanced than those of the other countries. Chinese consumers moved away from using credit cards to digital wallets, such as Alipay. Alipay is the most popular e-Wallet used in China as well as Asia with one billion users. In China, you can use Alipay to pay for almost anything. Such tools as Alipay speed up the transactions and increase customer confidence. PayPal is a similar system used in the West, though not as widely used as Alipay.

E-commerce platforms such as Shopify which are integrated with social media platforms make it easy for brands to reach their target audiences.

Adapting for the local markets

As it is in the nature of Globalisation, transnational companies have resources to adapt themselves for local markets. And let's not discount their vision and desire to satisfy customers. A good example of this is Pizza Hut's offering afternoon tea packages in China. This shows that they are ready to adapt to satisfy demand in local markets and create or amend their products to suit the tastes of local customers.

This changes the game and in order to compete for this level of adaptation, SMEs must adapt a similar viewpoint. Dedication to customer service will fuel an increase in their sales and reach.

The cost of not being part of a global economy

It is vital for the survival of SMEs to keep up with the latest trends in current economic developments. This applies regardless of their global ambitions. A local sandwich shop may not have a vision for global expansion, but still will be adversely affected if Subway sets up shop in the area. If the local shop notices that they are losing their customers to Subway too late, it will be very difficult for them to compete and survive.

This means they run the risk of losing their years of hard work.

If you are one of these companies that is already trading globally, then you can skip this chapter and move to the next chapter where you will find tools and tips to help you to improve your reach and your bottom line.

You have already gone over the perceptions and overcome the initial difficulties and established relations that have enabled you to start trading globally. You should congratulate yourself and the team behind it as you are one of the small percentage of the UK's SMEs in the export market.

Is it reasonable or logical to suggest that thinking international trade is a must for SME growth and its survival in some industries? It is important that SME executives have a mind shift where they see global trade for their long-term survival. Companies that stop growing have a high risk of sliding backwards and may end up disappearing altogether.

Many micro and small business owners feel that globalisation is posing a threat to their survival. However, this is a pessimistic viewpoint and should not be taken as an indication that SMEs need to take a different path in their marketing and sales activities to any other company. It takes a mindset shift to accept that size is not the decider and act accordingly.

Case study - Delivery Hero & Yemeksepeti

The Turkish start-up 'Yemeksepeti' (Food Basket) was established in 2001 in Turkey to serve the Turkish market. It became the third-biggest food delivery platform in the world after the USA and UK in terms of country reach. In 2015, the world's biggest food delivery company Delivery Hero acquired it for a record amount of $589 million. It was the largest acquisition made in the online food ordering sector. Yemeksepeti still operates under the same brand name.

At the time of the acquisition, Yemeksepeti was processing over 3 million orders each month mainly in its domestic markets Turkey and 6 countries in the Middle East. Had Yemeksepeti had any more global reach at the time, its value would have gone up considerably as it would have been a much better fit with Delivery Hero's global strategy. Notably, because Delivery Hero has simultaneously acquired Greek market leader e-Food.gr.

Yemeksepeti, like most startups, has purely focused on its domestic market. This was articulated by one of the founders of the company that, 'Yemeksepeti' did not have any plans to grow globally from the start. This would have been the biggest differentiator for its valuation.

Global expansion is often overlooked by startups as well as established companies. Examples have shown over and over again that, when a company has a global reach its valuation goes very high. Later in the book we will look at the 'born global' concept.

Perceived difficulties of global trade

Let's be realistic, anything unknown to us we are likely to perceive as difficult. This is not any different to losing weight or increasing our fitness levels or speaking in public. It is often the case that we quickly forget about the perceived difficulty once we start tackling the task ahead of us.

Global trade is not any different in this sense. Some of the concerns may be:

- My business is too small to go global
- I have not got the time to go global
- How will I know if my product is suitable for global markets?
- It is too risky for my business.

The level of concern varies depending on where you are on the global trading journey. Fundamentally, a global trade is no different than trading in your domestic market. But it opens the door to new customers and that enables you grow. You simply replicate your product or service that you have already developed for your home market.

There are many examples that companies do not experience real growth until they start trading globally.

Before you start your planning it's wise to take a step back and assess where you are in your global expansion journey. Which of these statements describes you best?

- Not interested in global trade
- Interested, but with no steps taken
- You are aware of a country or countries where your product or service is in demand and you are considering how to reach these customers
- You are selling to another country via your website, but do not have a structure for selling globally yet
- You have been selling globally and finding that you have been increasing your turnover and profitability
- Selling globally is an integral part of your revenues and you are looking for ways to improve it all the time.

From our experience dealing with many clients, we find that the companies that get the most out of global trade have one or more of the following:

- They have a marketing department, and the department is responsible for home market as well as the other countries. In some large companies they may have managers responsible for different markets
- Their sales department works closely with their overseas distributors/agents and they listen to their feedback

- They have sales and product brochures in foreign languages
- Their marketing strategy includes exhibiting internationally
- They have a budget for translations
- They have someone responsible for managing translations
- They have a system in place for foreign languages document management
- They have systems in place to respond to any overseas enquiries promptly.

How to beat procrastination

You may have many reasons for being reluctant to take those first steps towards international trade. Particularly for small businesses with limited human and financial resources, it is easy to get absorbed in the daily routines and unintentionally neglect the main growth areas in the business. There is always a reason why to delay - and that's usually a fear of the unknown.

One of my motivations for writing this book is to demonstrate that international trade is possible for even micro-sized businesses. All it takes to get started is a structured model. That's why I created the 5-step LINGO model. It will help you to research and pinpoint opportunities. It shows you how to remove the 'unknown' and then get started in a structured way.

The simple, 5-step LINGO model is based on:

1. **L** for Learn the Market – (Research)
2. **I** for Information Gathering - (Analyse)
3. **N** for Navigate the Market - (pre-implementation)
4. **G** for Go Operational - (Implement)
5. **O** for Open for Business - (Monitor)

How much is procrastination costing you?

Procrastination can take place in any of the 5 stages. The higher the stage you are in, the higher the cost will be. If you are not involved in international trade, then the cost is in the lost opportunities.

This loss will not be visible, as it will not appear on your balance sheet.

The other cost is that you may have taken some steps, but left it halfway through. It is likely that the initial spending will not be beneficial anywhere else and it will be money wasted.

If this is the case, your time will be lost as well as your motivation.

Reluctance to act can result in one of the following:

- Losing potential customers: If you already have generated interest in your products, but are slow to follow through, it is very likely that customers will start looking elsewhere to satisfy that interest

- Losing market share: Once the opportunity is apparent, then it is very likely that other companies will follow suit. This could easily cost you your market share

- Wasted time and money on preparations: Preparations take time and cost money. Market research, making contacts, often involving external parties such as lawyers, marketing professionals, etc., soon add to costs. Some of this information will be time sensitive. In other words, after a certain period of inactivity, these searches need to be re-started as the marketplace changes continuously

- Losing motivation to continue in the future: This is probably the most critical cost for medium-sized companies. Initiatives like going global always come from the top. If you lose your motivation for any reason, then it is likely that global ambitions will come to a stop, and this is why it is likely to be the highest cost. You will be the driving force of an important initiative for the company and your motivation affects everyone else in the company.

Case study – A medium-sized company missing out on growth

This is a UK-based company that provides water treatment systems with an annual turnover of $30 million.

They get 20% of their revenues from their home markets and 80% from their global sales which span more than 25 countries.

It is an established company with a solid financial standing and satisfied customer base globally as well as in their home market.

Their products have local language versions of the user guides, but their website is in the English language only.

They receive regular requests from their export markets for information in local languages.

The company has been considering websites in other languages for a while, but has not been able to move forwards with the plan.

Most of their competitors have websites in multiple languages.

After doing research into their website and talking to various people from the company, we have discovered the following:

- *The company's website has hundreds of pages of content as well as many pdf files*
- *The company has a wide range of products available*
- *Their website team are always busy and have no spare capacity for any other work.*

On top of that, their website is not doing particularly well in Google searches. Any SEO improvements could mean more sales for them both in the UK and overseas.

The company is well-known in the UK, but they appear in the second page in searches for their main product. In their main European market, they only appear through their distributor and their distributor's web pages have outdated information.

There is clearly no quick-fix and this situation has been the reason they have delayed the localisation. As a result losing potential sales and missing out on reaching new customers.

Let's have a look at the possible options for them and see which one would be most suitable for their export strategy.

What are the localisation options?

Option 1: Translate everything on the UK website

Option 2: Create micro websites for each country

Option 3: Check Google analytics and translate only the top performing pages into other languages.

Option 1: Translate everything on the UK website.

Pros:

- No preparation time needed as all pages will be translated
- All languages will be consistent with each other

Cons:

- Pages and products that are not needed for the target country will be translated and this will be confusing for the visitors.
- Localisation will cost more
- It will take longer to get the websites to be available for the target audience.

Best practice: Review the content of the website first to make sure any duplicates are deleted, and any obsolete products are removed.

This will be a good exercise for the UK audience as well.

Option 2: Create micro websites for the languages

Pros:

- No high upfront costs as only products and pages needed will be translated for the target country
- It will be more target audience focused – resulting in a stronger call to action
- New pages can be added to it or it can be incorporated to the main site

Cons:

- Time element as initial preparation and content sorting needed
- Additional website domains to maintain

Option 3: Check Google analytics and translate only the top pages into other languages.

Pros:

- Cost effective for popular pages
- Remaining pages can be left in English (with 'hreflang' settings – hreflang tells Google which language the page is using)
- Expendable as the demand grows

Cons:

- Website will be dual language, which can be a little confusing for customers
- This may not be the best option if they are already selling in the target country.

Tip: 'hreflang' settings should be in place so Google does not penalise your site for duplicate content.

Best practice for website localisation

Considering the company's turnover of $32 million and 80% of this coming from global sales, the management's most logical option is to create a localisation strategy to ensure customer satisfaction and future growth.

It is remarkable that the company has achieved such growth without any native language support. It is a testament to the product and services they provide. Imagine the growth they would attain if they were engaging with potential customers in their own languages.

We address this in more detail on page 180.

Projections

Research has proven that companies who have language capabilities do 30% better than those who do not (ATC/Aston University research). Even if adding languages improved the annual turnover by 5%, it will mean $1.6 million additional turnover. It will cover the cost of localisation many times over.

According to research funded by Aston University and the Association of Translation Companies, it was found after analysing data from 415 completed surveys obtained from varies sizes of SMEs, 'companies embracing language capabilities are 30% more successful in exporting than those which do not'.

Source: LO-C 30 Report – Role of Languages in International Performance for UK SMEs

Case study – DJI Drones – Born global

DJI produces unmanned aerial vehicles with a turnover of $2.83 billion (2017) with offices in the United States, Germany, the Netherlands, Japan, South Korea, Beijing, Shanghai, and Hong Kong. The company website is available in 6 languages.

Founded in 2006 by Frank Wang, DJI's first prototypes were built in his university room, selling the flight control components to universities and Chinese electric companies. He moved to the industrial hub of Shenzhen and hired a small number of staff in 2006.

The company struggled at first and sold a modest number of components.

They gained greater momentum in 2009 by successfully piloting a drone around the peak of Mount Everest, DJI continued to grow in the 2010s and became a global brand.

DJI accounts for around 70% of the world's consumer drone market as of March 2020, with no other company accounting for more than 5%. What is the secret ingredient in DJI's global success?

DJI's global journey

DJI started with a creative and dynamic dream and a vision that embraced global trading. Headquartered in Shenzhen, widely considered China's Silicon Valley, DJI has benefitted from direct access to the suppliers, raw materials, and young, creative talent pool necessary for sustained global success.

Along with filmmaking, agriculture, conservation, search and rescue, and energy, DJI products are also being used by government institutions in some countries.

As of 2020, DJI products are widely used by U.S. police and fire departments and around the world to combat coronavirus.

With pioneering technology and competitive prices, DJI has been a truly global brand in less than 15 years; we can even say that it was born global.

Top 5 takeaways

1. For SMEs perceived difficulties can appear tougher to overcome than they really are

2. Globalisation is shaping trade in a multitude of different ways so it's wise to understand its impact on your own market

3. International trade gives you access to many more markets

4. Success in global trading depends on having the right tools for the job and being willing to adapt to local demands

5. Start-ups can be designed to go global from the very beginning.

Summary

It is fair to say that going global requires a global mindset. This applies to established companies as well as start-ups. In fact, it is much easier for a start-up to roll out to multiple countries from the beginning than an established company to move from trading nationally to internationally.

We are living in a globalised economy and thinking across borders will bring success at a much-accelerated rate.

Part Two: Going Global

It is no secret that global companies that embrace a global mindset perform higher than their counterparts.

In this section you'll get in a global mood, start to investigate the different aspects and become aware of the potential for your business. This will prepare you for working through the 5-Step LINGO model.

You will explore how to develop and how to communicate effectively in an international marketplace. Communicating locally doesn't always prepare you for the pitfalls of international communication; there are many examples of companies who have got it wrong. You'll work through the steps that will overcome communication barriers, so they don't hamper your company's progress at a later stage.

Then you'll be ready to get started on the 5-Step LINGO model in Part 3 of the book.

Chapter 4 First Things First

Now that you are motivated to expand into new export markets and want to explore how it could work for your business, let's get started.

Going global requires solid groundwork on which you can build a successful export business. The most important building block will be your mindset. This mindset will help you overcome the initial difficulties. Once you develop your global mindset and learn some of the habits of the biggest global brands, selling internationally will become an integral part of your business operation.

The next step is to develop a global mindset and be aware of potential entry barriers to your plans to go global. You will also need to consider some of the legal and practical issues you are likely to face as you start your global journey.

Possible entry barriers

There will inevitably be entry barriers for any new market, whether it is domestic or international.

Below are some of the main barriers you are likely to come across:

Geographical distance

Distance is an important factor as it has a direct effect on the cost of delivery. It is also important for product returns.

The geographical distance between the country of origin and the country to which you're exporting impacts the time to be spent on transit. For some goods this can be an important factor, especially when sea-freight is the only cost-effective option.

> *Example: Tesco brings their wines from South Africa in tankers and it's bottled in the UK to save money on transport costs. The transporting bottled wine would cost a lot more. This is something only a giant grocery company can do as they are able to finance all sections of the process.*

Political factors

Political turmoil makes planning and budgetary matters difficult. A stable political regime is a sign of a good economy and makes planning so much easier. This means that you need to be aware of the political as well as economic climate in the countries you plan to do business with.

Cultural and language factors

Cultural factors play an important role in consumers' approach to products. Therefore, it is critical to make an in-depth analysis of these factors in relation to the product you will be marketing in the new country.

Language matters even more. If people do not understand the information about a product, they are less likely to be interested in it.

Labels, leaflets, packaging, marketing material and advertising all need to be in the local language to give you the best chance of success.

Legal requirements

Legal requirements can change from country to country. This can affect the packaging, labelling and marketing information.

To prevent any unexpected costs, it is important to discover what is required and any legal costs before the roll out and include them in the cost projections.

Some of the entry barriers can be the result of having to deal with something unfamiliar. It's natural to be cautious about treading on new ground, but it's ground others have journeyed through before so it's not an impossible mountain to climb. In most cases it's simply a case of working through unfamiliar requirements systematically – or getting advice from someone with experience.

I have come across people that talk about far away countries with warmth and sympathy because they had an opportunity to spend time there. The country is familiar and they are happy to go back there. For the very same country other people may have a totally different perception based only on what they have heard in the media, online or from their connections.

I believe that we create some of the barriers ourselves based on hearsay or not-so-reliable information sources.

Typical barriers to trading with a new country are:
- Country is politically unstable
- Currency exchange rates are volatile
- There is no UK representation there
- The country is not part of any global economic treaty
- Product requirements are very different from our home market
- Strong local competition

- Different business cultures that will impact on how service-based industries operate in a new territory.

The above are typical barriers we come across working with many customers from different industries.

Global mindset – your first step to global success

It is no secret that we live in a globalised world. We no longer see anywhere as being too far or anyone too foreign – especially while doing business. Being successful in your local market is no longer enough. Most executives who are looking for growth would consider expanding their business internationally.

A global mindset can be defined as the ability to recognise and adapt to different cultural signals from different backgrounds and to be able to collaborate and work with them successfully.

Developing a global mindset requires you to comprehend both yourself and your surroundings. Once you understand your sense of work, your style of leadership and your team, and develop cultural awareness, you can easily adapt to diverse working environments and achieve success. In short, a global mindset is related to self-development.

The first step to global success is having a global mindset. A global mindset can help you develop the necessary skillset for doing international trade and your global mindset will create an organisational transformation, resulting in an organisational global mindset.

The three steps below will help you understand how this whole process works in practice and develops this mindset. After all it is a skill that can be learned.

1 Be aware of your own cultural preferences

We are all a product of our surroundings, environment and families. Everything we experience and learn throughout the years shapes our preferences. Whether this is a business culture, family culture or national culture, there are many factors affecting our biases and shaping our understanding of style.

Although it can be quite difficult to understand and feel comfortable with our own cultural preferences, it can be a useful practice to learn about other people's cultural preferences and differentiate what makes them different from or similar to our own.

Having a clear definition of our cultural preferences is an excellent first step towards a global mindset.

2 Recognise that other cultures will have different values

There is no right or wrong when it comes to culture. Some cultures value loud and warm interactions while some prefer a polite distance. In some cultures, the family is the centre of the whole society and valued above all while in some cultures, individualism is widely recognized as a valued trait.

None of these are better or worse than any other, they are simply different from each other. And with billions of people on this planet, it is not difficult to figure out that there is a myriad of cultures.

Keeping an open mind and welcoming different cultures with enthusiasm and curiosity rather than judgement and prejudice is extremely important for reaching a global mindset.

3 Develop a strategy to learn and adapt to different cultural styles

Even smaller units like family and friend groups can have strong impacts on shaping our cultural understandings let alone bigger factors like nation and country. It is the same for everyone and that is what makes us feel different from the rest of the world sometimes.

Once you learn about your cultural preferences, understand different value systems throughout different cultures and process your knowledge you will start to recognise culture-based actions. Then you will need to develop your own strategy to adapt to various cultural styles.

Some cultures might be closed, while some are open to interactions. Some may find the way you do business to be strange, while some think that it is perfectly normal. Once you recognise the reason for different behaviours is based on cultural differences and not personal, you will find it easier to adapt to new export markets quickly and be much more successful.

A global mindset requires open-mindedness, understanding and curiosity. Leaders with a global mindset are usually very curious about different cultures, their surroundings and how to use all these information to improve themselves as more successful leaders. They usually appreciate differences and celebrate diversity.

Global learning comes with constant learning and development and leads to a global mindset and international success in the end.

New market entry strategies

Depending on the new export market, your product and your sales strategy, you need to choose the most suitable way to get your products launched.

Whether you are selling B2B (business to business) or B2C (business to consumer) will have a bearing on this decision. There are several market entry methods depending on whether you are offering products or services.

Before we look into exporting options let's briefly detail some of the other market entry methods:

- **Licensing:** If you have an intangible product or service based business, licensing could be a viable method for you. Here the licensee will pay your company a fee to use your trademark, intellectual property, or a model you have developed. If you choose this method, you need to make sure your intellectual property is protected in the new market.

- **Franchising:** This is somewhat similar to licensing, but strict franchise rules will apply as effectively a franchise is a 'business-in-a-box' and it's important that your franchisee follows the systems properly. You will need to investigate how to protect your system and brand in the new market.

- **Joint ventures:** Your business can establish a jointly-owned business with a compatible local business to serve the new market. There are several benefits with a joint venture, but it requires a different kind of due diligence. There are many aspects you need to take onboard before choosing a compatible company. Remember that business cultures will be different and you need to understand these thoroughly so they don't form a barrier - or a stumbling block in future.

Exporting

Exporting is the most common method of entry into a new market. This means your production is carried out in your current facilities and the products are then sent to the new market. There are couple of different ways to export.

Indirect route - Export management companies

With this method your company will not be directly involved in the export activities.

Export management companies can play a crucial role when there are strict export regulations and when travel restrictions are in place. They can provide you with support in logistics, customs clearance and even with distribution.

Research and consultation to find the most suitable and cost-effective option is important and it is advisable for you to spend time on this.

At the time of writing of this book it is not possible for international travellers to visit China due to the COVID-19 pandemic travelling restrictions. If your company had already planned to expand to China, then using a reputable export management company will be the only option available to you. For such markets as China, it may be a good idea to engage with such companies from the beginning so that you can account for their service costs as well.

It is best not to change course due to the pandemic (or any other major event that may impact your plans), as long as your budget allows you to do so. Even if it means lower profits, it may still be good practice to go ahead with your global plans despite this kind of restriction.

If these activities don't result in trading at a loss, it can be a smart move to go ahead when others (your competitors) are holding back. Consider a lower level of profits as an investment for the future. Customer loyalty does not happen overnight.

Distributors

Distributors in the new market, will hold your stock and fulfil orders. Unlike agents or representatives, they set the prices themselves and they oversee the import/export process themselves.

You need to find the best way to work with your distributor to suit your business. For instance, agreements about exclusivity and returns need to be agreed at the beginning. You will need legal agreements with overseas distributors to protect both parties.

Direct market entry

This method involves exporting directly to your customer. If your product requires little need for after-sales care or for servicing this may be more suitable for you. This is also more suitable when you may have a niche product with a limited customer base.

If you choose to export directly you may need to:

- Find representatives or agents in your new market
- Make arrangements for shipping and documentation
- Do your own market research for setting your prices.

Online marketplaces

There are over 50 online marketplaces operating globally and the number is growing. These platforms range from selling a wide range of products to some of them being specialist, focusing on cetin product ranges such as electronics or home and garden products or clothing.

There are also some marketplaces operating in a single country. It is important to be aware of these marketplaces.

Here are some benefits of why marketplaces can be useful:

- Easy to set up
- Access to large audiences
- Access to international markets
- Help with marketing
- Data and analytics
- Payment collections
- Fulfilling deliveries and dealing with returns.

When you are trying to get into a new export market, you are likely to face a few challenges and there are many things you need to discover in order to sell there successfully. In this respect, using an online marketplace can provide an easy and convenient solution.

According to Statista, over a fifth of online shopping sales in 2022 will be generated internationally and the largest e-commerce markets are still showing average growth rates between 6 and 10%, notably France, South Korea, Germany, UK, Japan, USA and China.

There are global online marketplaces that cover many different products and some are subject specific. Some will operate globally covering many countries and some are country specific or maybe covering just a small number of countries.

They all have different fee and commission structures. Therefore, choosing a suitable marketplace is important to ensure a successful start. Also, it may be a good idea not to use several marketplaces at the start. Each platform will require attention, fine tuning listings take time and there is also a danger of not being able to fulfil orders as your stock may be divided between marketplaces.

Some online global marketplaces

There are household names such as Alibaba, Amazon and eBay. These are global marketplaces providing off the shelf solutions for any business that would like to sell cross-border.

Amazon European Marketplace

Amazon provides a lot of data for similar products to yours where you can research competitors' prices, positioning and even their reviews. Once you are satisfied that you have a product suitable for this platform then it's time to go global – digitally.

Once you have an Amazon seller's account, you can benefit from Amazon's European Marketplace, selling to 5 European countries. FBA (Fulfilment by Amazon) is worth considering for the European countries as Amazon handles all deliveries and returns. Amazon is a massive platform, where the buyers search for the products they are looking to purchase.

Top Tip for Amazon

Search terms change from country to country. It is important that your team carries out thorough research, making sure that your product appears under the most popular search terms for your product. Therefore, product descriptions should be localised for each new market and not directly translated to the language.

There are also established online marketplaces in most countries. Therefore, it is important to be aware of them so that you are not just limited to the likes of Amazon, eBay or Etsy. (refer to Chapter 4 for more details)

TIP: You need to do research to establish the platforms suitability for your brand. If you are selling textile products there may be some platforms more suitable than others. Likewise, you need find the most suitable one if you have a technical product.

Amazon is far from the only online option, the following are some of the lesser known ones that may be more relevant, depending on your line of business.

The selection of marketplaces below is not an exhaustive list.

Fruugo

http://www.fruugo.com
Fruugo is global platform available in 46 countries. It provides product listings in 28 languages using its own translation technology and operates on a 'no sale no fee' basis. You will need a GTIN (Global Trade Item Number) in order to use the Fruugo platform.

Linio

http://www.linio.com
Linio has 20 million registered users and is the largest online marketplace in Latin America covering Argentina, Chile, Colombia, Ecuador, Mexico, Panama and Peru. Canon, French Connection and GoPro already sell using this platform.

Newegg

http://www.newegg.com
Newegg is a top online marketplace for selling technology in the USA. They have 33 million registered users and serve India, Ireland, Netherlands and New

Zealand too. Known brands such as Acer, Belkin and Sennheiser sell there.

Spartoo

http://www.spartoo.co.uk

Spartoo is a household name in France and neighbouring countries, but little-known in the UK. They focus on clothing and shoes. To join the platform, the sellers need to have a minimum of 250 products, so it is not for everyone. Nevertheless, if your business is in clothing or shoes, then it is worth knowing about Spartoo as it has 450 million registered users.

Country specific online marketplaces

These marketplaces cater mainly for a specific country or are well-established in certain countries. This may be because of using a country's native language or a specific product range that is particularly attractive to the natives of that country.

Allegro

http://www.allegro.pl

This is a de facto online marketplace for selling in Poland. They have over 21 million registered users and sell a wide range of products, from fashion to electronics.

Flipkart

http://www.flipkart.com

Flipcart is India's largest online marketplace with 100 million registered users. They provide different types of fulfilment and they cover all major products.

Trade me

http://www.trademe.co.nz

With 4.4 million registered users, Trade Me is new Zealand's largest digital platform. Many UK brands already sell on this platform. A wide range of products are offered, ranging from home & living to consumer electronics.

Rakuten

http://www.rakuten.jp

Rakuten is a force to be reckoned with if you want to reach Japanese buyers. They have 105 million registered users and focus on a wide range of goods. Many Japanese buyers only speak Japanese, so Rakuten could be an ideal solution for raising brand awareness.

La Redoute

http://www.laredoute.fr/

With 11 million users La Redoute is France's popular online platform for fashion and homeware. They also have a presence in 26 countries.

Kaufland.de

https://www.kaufland.de

This online marketplace has over 5000 products lines and servers the German market. Kaufland.de belongs to Europe's biggest retailer, the Schwarz Group, and it is well-known in Germany. Products include consumer electronics, DIY, homeware and more.

Tmall and Tmall global

https://about.tmall.com/
Both brands are part of Alibaba Group. Tmall requires businesses to be established in China or have a Chinese trading partner, where Tmall Global is a cross-border marketplace and allows retailers to sell directly to Chinese consumers without operations in China.

Kaola

http://www.kaola.com
Acquired by Alibaba in 2019, Kaola.com presents western brands to the Chinese buyers. They have 30 million registered users and there are different business models to suit the sellers. If you are considering Kaola.com for your business, it is essential to study the available options and choose the most suitable option for your product.

Online marketplaces are a viable way to reach international customers. You need to make sure your product is suitable for an online marketplace to get the best out of them. It pays dividends if you research for unique marketplaces for each country and do not only limit yourself on main ones such as Amazon or eBay.

It is also important that you review product descriptions for each country making sure you use the popular terms for your products. For any countries with higher than normal returns, you need to look for marketplaces that handle returns as well.

Export success case study – Truede Ltd

Company website: https://www.truede.com/

Founded in 2003 by Zeynep Turudi to bring authentic Turkish Delight to the UK market. Truede sell their products in the UK and export to 10 countries worldwide. Currently 40% of their turnover comes from global sales. Truede's Founder, Zeynep Turudi (Ms), was awarded Export Champion in 2020 & 2021 by the UK Department of International Trade. 92% of the sales comes from B2B customers. Zeynep has also created healthy chickpea snacks that are now also offered to clients.

Post-Brexit situation

With Brexit finalised, it became apparent that Truede products sold in EU countries would face a 22% export levy as their product of origin is from Turkey. Practically this will make the EU market unprofitable for the company. Previously, 15% of the turnover was generated from the EU market. Truede is now focusing on non-EU markets for growth.

The Opportunity

With an established range of its Turkish Delight products and a new healthy snacks product, the company is well placed to grow its customer base, by focusing on its current B2B customers. In addition, they now market their products to consumers via Amazon, eBay and Etsy e-commerce platforms.

Five habits of global brands worth adapting

There are lessons to be learned from the major global brands. Most of them have got to the stage they are currently at by following strict structures and often with business plans that require nerves of steel!

I would like to mention these briefly and some of them may be useful or inspirational for you. After all, we need to learn from experiences of others.

So, what **ARE** the five habits?

Habit number one: Global brands are growth orientated from the start

Intentionally successful major brands grow exponentially right from the start. This growth is not accidental. The growth is planned and executed to the letter and this is a common habit all major global brands exhibit. If you look for example at Uber, Airbnb, Samsung and Apple – they are different businesses, in different sectors and with different client bases but, there is a common thread when it comes to growth orientation and embedding that into business operations from day one.

Habit number two: Global brands are driven by a global mindset

The brands who have successfully grown globally tend to see the world as one big marketplace. They do not constrain themselves to their domestic market or limit their thinking to their national borders. They see the world as a connected, expansive marketplace – this is absolutely vital in the age of the Internet, where physical restrictions are removed and brands, products and services from the opposite hemisphere are readily available with the click of a mouse or tap of a smartphone screen.

Habit number three: Global brands have local language versions of their website

Connecting with consumers from other countries means you need to converse with them in their language. This is what major brands do well. Whether you're a customer in Korea, a shopper in Germany or a customer in the Middle East, you can go to the Lego website, read information in your own native language and pay in your local currency. It is a comfortable, reassuring and seamless experience.

Habit number four: Global brands enable their customers to make purchases in their local currencies

Broadly speaking, all successful brands trading internationally accept payments in the local currency. There are some exceptions to this rule, but very few. The exceptions generally accept standard Euro or US dollars. So there's no complicated currency exchange for customers or danger of customers being unhappy because the price they paid has changed due to currency fluctuation.

Successful global brands enable their customers to make purchases in their local currencies.

Habit number five: Global brands create products for the local markets

Another common trait is the creation of products for the local market or, existing products are amended to better suit the local markets. In other words, successful brands don't have one product that they try to sell across the world. They make the necessary amendments. KFC is a great example of this. In Shanghai for example, they sell afternoon tea. That's unheard of in Western Europe, but relevant to the Chinese consumer. Dunkin Donuts take a similar approach, they have a special donut developed especially for the Chinese market.

I believe that if small to medium sized companies can adapt and adopt these five habits and mindset, it will fuel and accelerate their global growth; an essential part of any sales or business development activity.

Business Insight

According to research by McKinsey, growth matters more than ever during times of challenge. It says that "opportunities will not always come in traditional or even familiar locales; indeed, from 2010 to 2025, almost 50 percent of global GDP growth will take place in approximately 440 small and medium-sized cities in emerging markets."

That is real food for thought and underline the importance of expanding globally rather than relying on a single market.

Case study – Brompton Bikes – Creating a product for the global audience

Brompton is a UK company with a turnover of £42 million (2019), they design and manufacture folding and electric bikes.

Brompton's production started in 1981. Up until 2002, they produced 6000 bicycles. After Will Butler Adams joined the company their production went from 6000 to 40,000 units per year and the workforce increased from 24 to 190. Their international sales were the biggest contribution to this increase.

Brompton is a classic example of how an executive can make a difference to an already successful brand by taking it to global markets. Today, Brompton is the largest volume bicycle manufacturer in Britain, producing approximately 40,000 bicycles each year. They offer 16.5 million combinations on the bike, every one of which is still made by hand in London.

Brompton holds the Prince Philip Designers Prize, The Queen's Award for Export and the Queen's Awards for Enterprise, and Managing Director, Will Butler Adams, has been awarded the Order of the British Empire (OBE). Today they have 10 stores in Asia and Europe and sell to 44 countries worldwide. With the help of these 10 stores, which opened only in the last 10 years, their sales has been going up dramatically. Brompton now sells over 45,000 bikes each year and there are estimated to be 80,000 Brompton bikes being used just in London.

Top 5 takeaways

1. It's important to be aware of any entry barriers to your chosen export market

2. A global mindset needs to be learned to be successful

3. There are many different market entry methods and it's important to research thoroughly so you choose the one that is best for your company and situation

4. Country-specific online marketplaces can be very useful to test the market and must be researched individually using the local popular search terms

5. Growth will not always come from traditional locales.

Summary

Today, growing globally is no longer a luxury, it's a necessity. Interestingly, it has become a reality for small and medium-sized companies with the advancement of logistics and payment gateways.

I believe that you can develop a global mindset and adopt the same habits used by major global brands to accelerate your business's global growth and make international success a reality.

Chapter 5 International Communication

When most executives and business owners think about going global they seem to automatically first consider English speaking countries, as they assume there will be no cultural or language barriers.

Even between English speaking countries there can still be language and cultural differences that, as an executive driving this growth, you need to be aware of. Marketing campaigns based on assumptions can be very costly when it comes to different countries even when you share the same language.

For example, in Canada when they talk about a 'buggy', they mean a different product than what is mostly meant in the UK. What is a 'boot' in the UK is a 'trunk' in the USA. 'Dustbin' in the UK is a 'garbage can' in the USA, 'trousers' are 'pants' and the list goes on.

George Bernard Shaw famously said 'England and America are two nations separated by a common language'.

If it is possible to have misunderstandings, even in the same language, imagine the number of things that can go wrong between different cultures.

Cultural factors are as important as the language as they form the basis of any written or spoken communication.

Hand gestures, and even silence have different connotations in different cultures.

Hand gestures are a sign of a dispute or aggression in some cultures. Personal space, forms of address, eye contact all need to be interpreted differently depending on the culture. Not being aware of these differences can prevent the start of a good relationship or even kill the possibility of cooperation before the foundation is laid.

It should not be taken for granted that the materials you have for the UK market will be suitable for the other English-speaking markets. These materials, whether packaging, user guides or marketing, should be edited and made suitable for the target countries, otherwise, it can lead to misunderstandings.

What is international communication?

International communication is how we accept and adapt to other countries' culture in a way that is comfortable for them. As we live in the age of globalisation, effective international communication is the key to successful cooperation.

Even though English is the lingua franca of business in many parts of the world, recognising the cultural differences is very important for effective and successful communications. If these are not recognised, the underlying differences can create barriers to effective or successful outcomes.

The sound of silence

In verbal communication it is critical to observe and recognise different cultural norms.

In the Far East silence is not passive it is active. In this context, silence is used for observation, setting the scene, getting to know each other, and giving the other party room to settle down.

In Anglo-Saxon conversations, when the one person stops the second person speaks. It is impolite to interrupt the other person. In Latin culture this doesn't apply. Frequent interruptions are a sign of an interest in other person's conversation, not a sign of disrespect.

This changes a quite a bit for Far Eastern cultures. When the first person stops speaking, the second person does not start immediately. For a western person this could be interpreted wrongly as a sign of failure to communicate. However, for this culture it is simply their way of processing information before starting to speak.

International communication is about communication across borders. Therefore, it needs to be taken seriously, as success depends on recognising and respecting cultural differences.

It's not what you say, it's the way that you say it!

It is scientifically proven that, during verbal communication, the tone of your voice has more impact than the actual words used. Even in your domestic market, the tone of voice is the main differentiator for getting your message across to your potential customers.

This carries a lot more weight when it comes to cross-border communication. Along with the intricacies of a different culture, your tone of voice can make or break a relationship. Some cultures are informal and respond well to a chatty, friendly approach, others are more formal and expect business conversations to be based on respect and a professional persona. If you don't understand the culture your deal may be dead in the water before you get to draw up the contract.

7 tips to avoid cross cultural misunderstanding

1 – Do not jump to conclusions about their intention

During a meeting something they said or made a comment about may come across to you as offensive or rude. You may feel that way from the tone of voice or the body language. This is where you take a deep breath and assume they have good intentions.

In some cultures, it is not unusual to ask personal questions such as your age, marital status, and about your family members. Be prepared so that you don't misinterpret these questions.

2 – Always ask clarifying questions

Asking clarifying questions will help to stay on course and prevent any misunderstanding.

Potentially any critical numbers, dates, details may be misunderstood. It will be extremely helpful to clarify them with your counterparts. You can confirm what you understood and confirm what you have agreed with your counterpart. Get into the habit of summarising what actions need to be taken so that there is no ambiguity later.

This goes both ways; what your counterpart says or suggests may appear to be completely outside the parameters of your contact with them. If this is the case the only way to get to the next stage is to ask tactful clarifying questions without implying that they have misunderstood you.

3 – *Show you value and respect them*

It is important that you make it clear to them that you value them as your counterparts in the meeting or in the negotiation you are part of. The tricky part here is that, when you are not familiar with the culture, there is a risk of offending them without realising you have done so. Observing your participants in the meeting, showing empathy could work in your favour.

The sooner you understand the dynamics of the room, the better position you will be in to avoid any unintentional mistakes. For example, taking off your jacket during the first meeting, or addressing someone by their first name may come across disrespectful. Observing the room and being aware of expectations ahead of the meeting will work to your advantage.

4 – *Never make assumptions*

When you are working cross culturally, it is best not to trust your intuition. The only way to overcome this is to carry out thorough research about the culture you are interacting with. Just because you are happy to be addressed by your first name, do not assume that they will be happy with that too. First name basis may come at a later stage in the relationship.

Some cultures can be sensitive on subjects that you feel totally neutral about. This could be to do with politics, history, religion and even football in some countries where football is an integral part of life. Making a remark about one of these subjects can come across as offensive and, once said, it's very difficult to back-track.

5 – Slow down

Native speakers who are excited about the subject often speak faster. This seems to be the case in any language. When you are dealing cross-culturally and you are addressing them in English, which is not their native language, slow down and make sure you use plain English without any jargon, metaphors or slang that can only be understood by the native speakers.

6 – Avoid humour

Many of use humour to break the ice at the meetings or use it to increase engagement. In international settings it is best to avoid humour as humour doesn't always work in other cultures or things can get lost in the translation. In the worst case scenario, it may be offensive and can become a deal breaker. If you really want to use humour, make sure you carry out your research and use it with caution.

7 – Mirror the body language of the person or people you are in the room with

You can observe the body language of the person or people you are with and use that to help you communicate effectively. What is their take on personal space, are they leaving a big gap between themselves and the person they're talking to? Are they using any hand gestures? How loud are they speaking to each other? Is there anyone in the room that everyone is paying particular interest or respect to?

Cross-cultural communication takes work and the time spent in learning what is expected – and what you can expect – will pay off in successful negotiations.

Some points to consider for international communication

- Have you researched the culture of the new market?
- Do you know their take on age and gender?
- Do men and women shake hands?
- Do they do anything differently with an older person?
- What is their communication style? (direct or reserved)
- How do they use hand gestures?
- What is their take on gift giving or gift taking?
- Is it rude to turn down a drink offer?
- What is their approach to timekeeping? (i.e. strict or relaxed)
- What is their approach for meeting etiquette (i.e. taking calls during meetings)
- What does silence mean in the culture?

You can download our international communication checklist from ttcwetranslate.com/book/checklists

Germany's famous jelly doughnut

Did you know that Germany's famous jelly doughnut is known by at least three different names in different regions?

People of Brandenburg, Western Pomerania and Saxony know them as 'pfannkuchen'. In southern and central Germany, they are 'krapfen'. For Northern and Western Germany, it is 'berliner'.

But for the past 60 years, jelly doughnut is not the first thing that comes to mind when someone says berliner; it's JFK's famous 'Ich bin ein Berliner' (I am a Berliner) speech given in 1963 in West Berlin. It was an honest mistake – he simply didn't know that one article made him a pastry, not a Berlin citizen.

He also probably did not know that 'berliner' referred to jelly doughnut as it's known as 'pfannkuchen' in and around Berlin.

The lack of cultural awareness can have huge implications and they may not always be as innocent as the 'berliner' example.

Using plain English

When it comes to international communication using plain English is one of the biggest differentiators. Interestingly, using plain English even makes it easier for the domestic audience to get your message most of the times.

You may have visitors coming to your website from different countries. English is still one of the widely-spoken languages on the Internet. But most of these visitors will be from different countries and therefore using plain English will enable them to get the information they are looking for without any ambiguity.

Once you know you have an international audience it is important to reach them with your content to keep them interested in what you are doing.

It is even more important if your content is to be translated into another language.

Plain English means using an easy-to-follow and easy-to-understand language so that your message can be conveyed effectively to your audience.

One common misunderstanding is that plain English means using beginner level English or choosing the simplest words. This is not the case. Plain English simply means using simple sentence structures, avoiding pompous language and obscure phrases, cutting out slang, jargon and metaphors or similes that may not work in other cultures.

Writing in plain English provides readability for a wider audience. By keeping short sentences and using familiar words, you can easily create a clear and consistent narrative and reach your audience. This may take time to review and edit what you want to say.

As Mark Twain once said, "I didn't have time to write you a short letter, so I wrote you a long one." Take the time to write a short, clear and concise presentation.

How to get it right

Before: The application must be completed by the applicant and received by the department by 2nd January.

After: We must receive your application by 2nd January.

What is a contract?

- A bible (USA)
- Prison (Italy)
- Words can be interpreted flexibly (France)
- Insurance document (Netherlands/UK).

Translating the slang

Let's get down and dirty to Americans means be honest and open

Can we table that item?

- English – can we discuss this?
- Americans – delete/ignore this item

We have tied up all the loose ends - non-native English speakers have no idea what this means

Confusing: I will get on to Susan and get her to get on with it

Better: I will ask Susan to do it straight away

We will get it done eventually – may not get the result you expect in France where 'eventually' means 'maybe'

That is quite good

- Americans – it means very good
- English – it is so-so.

You must not work after 6 o'clock to Germans means you do not need to work after 6pm, for English people it's more a command than a suggestion.

The delay in this project is 2 weeks

British people understand that the project is running behind by 2 weeks, while French 'delay' means 'lead time', so the project isn't behind at all!

Don't take it at face value:

In Germany – I disagree means exactly that, but in Britain disagreement is not always expressed directly so they might say "To be honest, I am not sure", and in Japan they may say "It is difficult".

Some idioms, for example, can be hard to translate from one language to another and even when they are translated, they can be easily misinterpreted in the target language. Avoiding the use of such idioms and colloquial terms, choosing words and phrases that leave no room for misunderstanding will make your text much clearer and easier to translate. Another point you need to take into consideration is the use of jargon or culturally-biased language. These can be misunderstood in your domestic market let alone an international one.

Using plain English will keep your content clear and consistent, leading to consistent quality translations. After all, a clear source text creates a clear target text and it increases the overall quality of communication by giving a reader a better understanding, and a better reading experience.

Here some steps you can take to make your content in plain English:

- Keep your sentences to within 20 words
- Choose words that are relevant for your audience
- Use active verbs wherever possible

- Think of your content as a source text for another language
- Don't use colloquial language
- Avoid culturally biased words and idioms.

What to do with your global partners

- Use direct, clear communication
- Be explicit about deadlines
- Use plain English
- There are no stupid questions
- Remember the Korean proverb, we have two eyes, two ears, one mouth for a reason.

Case Study – Amara Living - Growth by overcoming language barriers

Website: www.amara.com

Amara, based in Essex, UK, designs and produces luxury home accessories and furniture, they also collaborate with famous luxury brands. They have a turnover of over $44 million and have a 85-strong team.

The journey of Amara started with Sam deciding to redesign her own home and noticing a gap in the high-class interior design industry. Being passionate about interior design for a long time, she partnered with her husband to start what became Amara in 2005.

The physical store enabled them to build a solid clientele and establish Amara's style, but they decided to turn to e-commerce completely in 2008.

By making their website available in various languages and countries early on, including the Middle East, they secured their global audience and grew quickly. Focused on high-end luxury products, Amara has grown to partner with over 300 of the world's leading luxury home brands, including Versace Home, Missoni, Fornasetti, Roberto Cavalli and Kartell.

They have an award-winning customer care and a global audience in over 100 countries.

Amara's timeline

2005	Amara is founded by husband-and-wife team Sam and Andrew
2006	Website is launched in English
2013	Websites launched in AU and USA
2014	UAE website launched. French language version is launched. Turnover £5.3 million
2015	German language website is launched. Websites in Canada, New Zealand and Ireland are launched. Turnover £8.7 million
2016	Turnover is almost doubled to £15.5 million
2017	Turnover £18.9 million
2018	Turnover £21.2 million
2019	Belgian website launched. Turnover £21.9 million
2021	Saudi Arabian website launched. Turnover reaches £33.7 million

Source: Companies House Accounts

From the above table it is evident that Amara's growth is in correlation with reaching customers in their native languages.

Top 5 takeaways

1. Using plain English benefits your home customers as well as international customers
2. It is possible to overcome cultural barriers by recognising, understanding and respecting them
3. International communication requires a strategy
4. How you address language and cultural issues can make it or break it for you
5. Accessible websites create more revenue.

Summary

How you conduct international communication is likely to determine your cooperation with your customers as well as suppliers. As it involves intercultural relations, it is easy to get things wrong and ultimately affect relationships and lose potential business.

On the other hand, though, it is not rocket science. It requires respect and understanding of other cultures and detailed, focused study to understand it.

Now you've done your preparation you're ready to explore the LINGO model and how you can apply it to your business, whether you are already involved in international trade or looking to get started.

Part Three: Implementation - The LINGO Process

I am sure there are companies who have achieved global growth without any major planning or simply by accident. This has happened before and no doubt it will happen in the future too. However, if you believe you have an opportunity to grow globally, then the only way that will guarantee results is to manage and control the process.

Working with dozens of companies over the last 30 years, I have noticed that many executives have missed growth opportunities because they did not have a structure when expanding globally. One thing that strikes me about the successful global brands is their approach to selling globally. Brands such as Apple, Uber, AirBnB, Netflix treat each of their markets as if it is their only market and all of them get the same brand treatment and support. This ultimately enables them to connect with their customers on many levels.

Equally, any of these will alienate your customers:

- Users not receiving important or critical information in their native language
- Incomplete or sub-standard landing pages for the target country
- Providing inconsistent or poor local content.

Reacting to change is important and necessary, but not following a growth strategy can take longer and cost more due to the time it takes and the danger of missing out essential steps. With that in mind, I developed the LINGO model, which provides you with 5 simple steps that map out your journey for each of your target markets.

In the next 5 chapters we will cover the following so you can work through each step and then dip in and out as you need to during the implementation process:

Chapter 6 – Learn The Market

This explains what you need to know to evaluate the market potential. It will be beneficial for you if you are expanding into a new export market. The New Country Testing Kit and the Brand Name Checking guidelines will be particularly useful for this purpose.

Chapter 7 – Information Gathering

This outlines the general structure to research a new market or if you want to deepen your understanding of an existing market.

Chapter 8 – Navigate the Market

This is the process for going deeper into a specific market, exploring connections, regulations, cultural protocols and all the details you'll need to ensure your product or service is launched with a strong foundation.

Chapter 9 – Go Operational

This takes you from theory to practice where your product or service is now available in a new territory, with all the necessary support in place to ensure its success.

Chapter 10 – Open for Business

You are now operational in the new export market. This is where you put your KPIs in place to monitor your performance and growth.

Chapter 6 Learn The Market

If your home market isn't performing as well as you'd like, you may be considering expanding to new international markets. In this chapter, you will find a structure on how to shortlist a new export market and criteria to apply to do so.

Learn The Market step is critical as most failures in new markets happen due to missing this stage.

You'll explore what you need to know to evaluate the market potential. It will be beneficial for you if you are expanding into a new market or getting started. The 'New Export Market Toolkit' and the 'Brand Name Checking guidelines' will be particularly useful for this purpose.

It is essential that you find out all critical information about the market you would like to expand into. This is important whether the market is in a different city or another country. This exercise includes checking all the available economic data, their infrastructure, legislation, ease of doing business, government contacts and other important aspects.

If you are already in an export market, I hope you'll still find some hints and tips in this chapter to develop your operations further. The socio-economic conditions are rapidly changing, and these directly affect customers' purchasing behaviours. Companies who sell in different markets need to follow the trends and adjust accordingly.

You can also use this chapter to review the steps you have taken and assess if you need to revisit any of them.

The New Export Market Toolkit

This kit will enable you to find out if your product is needed in the target country and the market potential. This will save time and money before you make the investment and will help you to calculate your return on investment.

Speaking with an executive from an established industrial glue manufacturer, he told me that they are unlikely to get involved in selling to another country based on their recent experience in a Central European country. Further in our conversation I learnt that they lost money and motivation following their attempt to expand in that country. The packaging and transport costs were higher than expected and the sales were lower than their projections. This left a sour taste in their mouth and, as a result, the company's managing director instructed that they should only focus on the UK market.

Later, I learned that they had only carried out limited due diligence. Had they completed comprehensive research they would have entered the new market fully informed and would not have been disappointed.

We created our 'New Export Market Toolkit' exactly for this purpose. It prompts you to seek information and facts on many levels, so you can make informed decisions about the suitability of the country you intend to expand to.

You can download this checklist from ttcwetranslate.com/book/checklists

Using the 'New Export Market Toolkit' you will get an entry level report, this will help you to gauge the new market's potential, and decide whether to proceed to the next level or not.

There are 5 main areas that form the report:
1. Target country market trade stats and figures
2. Target market language and customs
3. Target market's ease of doing business
4. Keyword research for the target market
5. Google market trends

This is the information you'll need to explore:

Whether you compile this report yourself or get someone to do it for you, it is important that you have this information available to reach an informed decision.

Now let us have a look at each stage.

1. Target country market trade stats and figures

This section entails basic information about the country including:

- Population overall
- Main cities and their population
- UK exports and imports with this country
- Country's trading partners and UK contacts on the ground
- Ethnicity of the country – this will have a direct effect on how you present your product or service.

In some countries, cities may have great differences between them.

This is an important factor to consider and it could be relevant to the product or service you are offering.

All this information will help you to assess the suitability of the market. If there are many UK companies already trading in this market and the UK government has contacts on the ground this can be encouraging.

The country's population and income levels can also influence your decision.

Case study - Grocery delivery service going global

Website: https://getir.uk/

A grocery delivery service founded in 2015, promises to deliver essential groceries within 10 minutes, 24 hours a day.

The company is a Turkish start-up called 'Getir', which literally translates into English as 'bring it to me'. It has recently expanded its services to London. They are currently valued at $850 million and are expected to reach a valuation of $1 billion within this year.

The company offers to deliver anything from lettuce to cold beer in 10 minutes in selected cities in Turkey, the Netherlands, Germany and, recently, in London.

What makes Getir stand out from hundreds of other start-ups is the fact that it has gone global at a very early stage in its operations and this has attracted substantial investment from local and international investors.

2. *Target country language and customs*

It's essential to know the language or languages spoken in the region, local customs, business etiquette, social media culture, religious and national holidays.

Understanding common business customs, such as the most frequently used search engines and which social media platforms are popular can be relevant too.

It is so easy to bypass this kind of information and it may have an impact on your success.

It's easy to assume that what applies in our own country applies everywhere else. For instance, although Google search and Google Adwords is widely used in most countries, in Russia Yandex is more popular and in China Google is banned altogether.

In Germany Xing competes with Linkedin. As of 2019, they had up to 16 million members in the DACH area (Germany, Austria and the German-speaking part of Switzerland).

National and religious holidays can play an important role. During these periods business transactions can be slow or may even come to a halt or the demand may increase greatly.

It's important to know the differences between public holiday times in different parts of Europe.

For instance:

- 1st May is a public holiday in most European countries in celebration of International Labour Day
- Germany has regional holidays as well as national ones
- Mother's Day is always the second Sunday in May in continental Europe and Turkey, but much earlier in the UK
- Countries that are predominantly Muslim will celebrate Eid Al Fitr at the end of Ramadan and Eid Al Adha approximately 10 weeks later. Because of the different calendar these celebrations will move every year.

If you are in e-commerce then this information can help you prepare in advance.

Cultural differences in the same country

Even in a European country such as Spain, it is important to be aware of the regional differences. Barcelona, capital of Spain's Catalonia region, uses Catalan in addition to Spanish. This does not apply to the rest of the country. Catalonia is an autonomous community in Spain. Therefore, businesses are required to display important information in Catalan as well as Spanish.

If your product is intended for Spain and Barcelona is one of the target markets, then failing to understand the Catalan language and customs of the Catalonia region can be costly for you. This is also critical for you when you are on the ground.

For instance, it will help you to know that in Catalonia they support Barcelona football club and Real Madrid is their arch enemy!

This is the kind of information that you need to know about any new territory you plan to export to – it can make a significant difference to the success of your campaign.

Business etiquette

Business etiquette in the country is a very important factor for conducting successful business. This prevents many misunderstandings and will help you and your team to adapt to the business culture and not do anything that will damage your company's image in your new marketplace.

In some countries it is acceptable to take phone calls during meetings. If you are not aware of this, you can easily take offence at your host's action and jump to a wrong conclusion. Similarly, for some cultures small talk is necessary in order to get the real conversation started.

There are no right or wrongs when it comes to cultural issues. Therefore, it is critical to be aware of the cultural issues and the business etiquette of the country.

This can even apply to how you address your counterpart. In Germany, for example, it is usual to address the person with their surname unless they have asked you to use their first name. Punctuality is critical in some countries, but not so much in others. The list goes on.

The important factor here is that business etiquettes change from country to country and if you want your business to grow in this country it is paramount that you are aware of what is acceptable and what isn't and can pass this on to your teams.

3. Target country's ease of doing business

This information is probably the most relevant in relation to the development and success of your operations in a new country. The country's ease of doing business includes the level of bureaucracy, their regulations, how they manage conflict resolution, the process for setting up joint ventures, and the process for protecting your intellectual property. These will all play an important part in developing your business in that country. In some countries in particular industries, it is not possible to do business without a local partner and this can be strictly controlled by the country's authorities. If this is not suitable for your business, the sooner you are aware of it the better.

The state of the digital economy, the country's transport and internet infrastructure will all have an impact on your ability to trade successfully in this country.

The World Bank 'Doing Business' website provides annual reports on the ease of doing business in 10 categories for 190 economies (refer to our 'Further Reading' section). The report provides a list of countries that became less business-friendly due to the introduction of strict regulations, and lists economies with the most notable improvements.

Categories include, setting up companies, payment collection, connecting utilities and even dissolving a company. Overall, it is a very useful resource and it will be well worth your time to study each country you're targeting.

The right paperwork

When you deal with another country's authorities, your business will be bound by the rules and regulations of that country. It is important to investigate these as early as possible as this will influence your decision regarding whether this country is a good export market for you.

You will need to know:

- Whether the new export market is part of the double taxation agreement
- What the Corporation tax rate is in the country
- If it's tax efficient to establish a local legal entity
- If you need to register for VAT or equivalent tax
- If your product's country of origin will result in additional import/export charges.

There are many rules and restrictions, as well as different tax and duty rates when moving goods from the UK to the rest of the world. Also you will need certain documents when exporting. Some countries may require additional documents as well.

Check our 'Further reading' section for useful sections of the UK government website.

4. Keyword research

Doing keyword research for your product or service in the target country will provide information on the demand and the competition as well. Whether it is a product or service this is valuable information to have.

You know the volumes and number of hours necessary to break even. Understanding the current search volumes in that country will give invaluable data and you can conduct further investigation using this data as a starting point.

A keyword study can be carried out using free tools such as Google AdWords accounts or Ubersuggest. Also, use Yandex for Russia and Baidu for China. For other countries, find out the most popular search engine and use that for your research.

5. Google Trends

Google Trends is a service that analyses the popularity of top search queries in Google Search across various regions and languages.

Choosing a new export market

Choosing your new market will take time initially, but it's worth taking the time to ensure you have a strong chance of success. Sometimes an element of chance will play a big role, such as receiving an order request from a particular country.

This may make you aware of the opportunities there and open up the possibility of exporting there – that doesn't mean you should skip over the research stage, it's still important to know what you're stepping into.

There are many elements that will help you to choose a suitable market. Some businesses have made their decisions on data derived from Google Analytics (which can give you some interesting data if installed correctly). From there it is possible to see from which countries your website traffic is coming.

This could be a starting point. Then by carrying out further tests or applying certain fields it can be possible to assess the quality of the data and your business case can be based on this.

Once you know which country your visitors are coming from, you can create a landing page to create further engagement and assess whether there is enough demand to take it further.

Attending an exhibition to do with your industry, product or service as a visitor or as an exhibitor can often reveal interest from that particular country as well as seeing what competition there is.

Trade missions organised by various government bodies can serve the same purpose and you may even get support towards your expenses.

It goes without saying that there is a wealth of information on the Internet which will build up your profile of the target country.

These are just some of the ways you can conduct an export market analysis.

The main purpose of these activities is to shortlist a few countries for further research. However, it is possible that your first experience may not meet your expectations.

Create a business plan

The new expansion should be considered as a new business and needs to have a business plan.

A business plan for the new export market will help you to:

- Set your expectations and goals so you can measure progress
- Foresee any bottlenecks or potential pitfalls
- Clarify your business idea for going global.

This plan will also be instrumental if the business needs to borrow money for any reason. The business plan should include local competition and market research findings for your products or services.

Many established businesses do not have an up-to-date business plan for their existing business, so it's a good exercise to carry out for both current business operations and for planned export markets.

You can get a business plan done by working with your business advisors or you can refer to the resources listed in our 'Further reading' section.

'Fail to plan, plan to fail'

Planning every step of the operation is crucial. This will help you not to miss any detail, no matter how small it may look.

For example, according to statistics 90% of the product recalls are due to mistakes or missing information in packaging.

This is because in other countries there are different labelling regulations. For regulated products such as medical devices or food products, these requirements need to be established at the earliest stage possible to avoid any costly revamps later.

Be ready to adapt

Good examples of adapting to new marketplaces are McDonalds and Burger King. They have been doing home deliveries from the day they started their operations in Turkey, although this is a fairly new concept for the UK market. It is normal to buy beer in McDonalds in Belgium.

This is demonstrating that they know their local markets and respond to the market's expectations. Large businesses have always been pioneers in adapting their products for each market.

What if the majority of your global trade is with a single country or region?

It is a fact that nearly 50% of UK's exports go to EU countries. And most of the SMEs involved in global trade deal with EU countries directly or supply to companies who export to the EU. It is possible that some companies only rely on a single country or region for their export sales.

If there were to be any domestic problems in these countries or regions, it is likely that the business who supplies these countries would also be adversely affected.

Therefore, it is important that you carry out regular risk analysis and take corrective action when necessary. Looking into other export markets is a viable option too.

No sensible business would rely on a single customer in their home country – if that customer fails, it will take your company down with it.

The same applies to export markets. In the global economy SMEs can find suitable (and profitable) customers irrespective of the country location.

Case Study - Tangerine - using innovation to reach global customers

Website: https://tangerine.net/en/

The company was founded in 1989 by Martin and Melinda Darbyshire. Tangerine is an international design consultancy with studios in the UK, South Korea and Brazil.

Their website is available in English, Chinese, Japanese and Korean.

Tangerine gets 80% of their business from overseas clients and has worked in 5 continents. Their designs resulted in creating 20+ patents for their clients.

One of their most notable achievements is designing the world's first fully flat bed in business class in 2000 for British Airways.

Tangerine is a prime example of British design going global. Their motto is 'explain clearly how we can help you to grow market share, drive new business and maximise your return on investment through innovative strategic design'.

Their latest 'maskless travel concept' design, VisAir, for safe air travel in a COVID-19 world is a great example of their innovative approach.

I believe the global success of the Tangerine design consultancy is because they truly overcome the language and cultural barriers of their international audience.

This is evident through their employment of people from different countries, their websites being available in three other languages and their studios in South Korea and Brazil.

Brand name checking

Another essential part of preparing to enter a new market is brand name checking.

In the resources section you'll see a link to the Brand Name Checking worksheet.

If you're planning to launch a new brand and intend to operate in a global marketplace it's wise to ensure that your brand name:

- Is not misunderstood by speakers of other languages
- Does not have any negative connotations
- Is not hard to pronounce
- Has another meaning in the native language of the country
- Does not clash with another brand name that is already registered.

There are plenty of examples where brand names in one language have been seriously embarrassing in another. You really do not want a blot on your reputation – and all the expense and effort of rebranding and relaunching.

Brand name checking is a particularly good investment and a useful step even if you are not planning to go global. This will make sure that the brand name chosen for your new product is suitable for an international audience.

If there is a similar brand name to yours in the new export market, they may be able to stop your operations by preventing the use of a particular brand name in their market.

Unless your brand name is protected in that country, you will not be able to operate there.

There can be even errors even between neighbouring countries as has happened with no other than IKEA.

One of IKEA's products is small boxes called 'Knepp' and it means 'tricky' in Swedish. But in the neighbouring Denmark it is a profanity, which is far from the intended purpose of the product name.

You can download our Brand name checking checklist from ttcwetranslate.com/book/checklists

Case Study – Good example of a brand name checking

Our client is a large international brand consultancy based in Japan. The project involved multilingual brand name checking of 206 possible names and many more phrases and words associated with the product.

The client wanted to check 21 countries for all these names and phrases and requested two linguists for most of the languages.

Although more than one country may use the same language there are local versions to consider; for example, Algeria, Bahrain, Libya, Mauritania, Morocco and Yemen all use Arabic, but each has subtle differences in usage.

Ghana, Mauritius and Zambia all use English – but each country has their own version, almost like a dialect that must be accounted for. Rwanda needed everything checking for both Kinyarwanda and Swahili.

39 linguists, all native speakers for the target languages took part in the project.

In addition, there were some rare languages such as Dhivehi and Montenegrin, for which our project managers successfully found translators.

Top 5 takeaways

1. Understand your target country thoroughly

2. Ensure you know exactly what paperwork your target country's authorities will need

3. Create a business plan for your new territory – no shortcuts!

4. Adapt to local customs and customer expectations

5. Check that your brand name has no negative connotations.

Summary

Step one, Learn the Market, is the most important step towards finding a new export market. The research that goes into this step will shape the rest of the model.

There is often the temptation to skip or even shorten this step because of hearsay or other external information coming your way. You should pay attention to these comments, but also complete your own due diligence.

You have looked at all the export markets you had in mind initially and assessed them with the help of New Export Market Toolkit and decided which one is most suitable for your company.

This will help you to make good progress for this market as you have already removed countries from the list that may not have been suitable. Instead of a trial-and-error approach, which can cost you time and money, you know which export market is likely to be suitable for you.

It's time for the next step in LINGO - Information Gathering.

Chapter 7 Information Gathering

In the previous step you have shortlisted a new export market or markets. If you have more than one market in mind, it is advisable to apply the LINGO model one market at a time, however tempting it may be get started in multiple markets.

The information gathering step is where you discover the essential information about the new export market you would like to expand into. This will ensure that you are fully aware of the local expectations such as packaging, special labelling requirements, colour preferences, box quantity and more.

This is everything to do with the finding the way in the new market from storage to customer returns logistics. This ensures that there are no product recalls.

Your research will also help you calculate the true cost of deploying the product to the new export market, making sure there are no surprise costs.

It is important to mention that you are still exploring the possibility of winning a new export market and you can still carry out the research mostly from your desk.

This chapter outlines a general structure that you can apply to a new market or use to deepen your understanding of an existing market.

Identify the competition in the new market

Like the boxers meeting before a big match where they check each other out and assess their limits, you need to find out as much as possible about the local competition.

During the process of introducing your products to the new export market, customers will compare your products to those they are already using.

Doing your research will ensure you can meet or exceed your customer's expectations.

Case Study: Aldi and Lidl entering the UK

The German budget supermarket brands ALDI and LIDL positioned themselves quite differently to the existing supermarket chains when they entered the UK market.

Their offering initially met with resistance from the shoppers who were used to shop from the big 3 (Tesco, ASDA, Sainbury's).

Their positioning was not based on providing cheaper products that the established big 3 currently offered. They took a completely different approach, offering their unique products and a different customer experience altogether.

They disrupted the market and as a result their market share has grown over the years.

They managed to create a customer following that likes their unique products and the experience they provide. They offer good quality, but less-known products at better prices and with less fancy packaging, along with a different checkout experience.

If you are looking to win a new export market you can learn from ALDI's and LIDL's experiences even if you are in a totally different industry. How can you add value to the customer's experience?

Market research, market testing guidelines, political and legal considerations

Market research entails getting all the information necessary so you can delight your customers in the new market.

If you aim to delight your customers, then your research will continue until you have all the information you need to create a strong export plan.

As this is a new market for your company it is easy to miss certain customer behaviours, which may not exist in your home market. Try not to make any assumptions and keep an open mind at this step.

Depending on your product or service, your target audience may show different levels of resistance to a new product or may not easily move to a new brand or new service offering. That's why market research is critical, so you can gather comprehensive information about your new customers.

I recommend that you apply established market research principles and work with local companies who have experience in your industry.

Political considerations are likely to change depending on your product or service. You need to ask yourself what effect, if any, political changes are likely to have on your operations.

During my research for this book, a company executive informed me that they could no longer sell their products in a country, because their product originated from a country that was in conflict with the country he had been exporting to. Because of this, they could no longer export their products to this particular country. While the conflict continues between these countries, the executive in question now needs to find alternative markets.

The legal bit

Legal requirements can be different between different countries and in a few cases it may be not just a few extra forms, but be dramatically different. You need to find out if the legal issues are likely to affect your activities before you start trading there. Legal requirements can affect anything including product information, logistics and financial matters such as bank transfers. In the UK, commercial banking services have improved tremendously over a decade. Do not assume it will be the same in the new export market. How long the transfers take to process is likely to affect your operations if your funds are held up in accounts due to national holidays or anti-money laundering regulations.

For some legal requirements you may have to prove your identity quite differently in the new export market to the UK.

In some countries, notary public offices play an important role. Most company-related documents need to be approved by a notary public, otherwise these documents will not be accepted in these countries. This applies to any property related activities as well as opening a business bank account.

Document legalisation – Hauge Apostille Convention

The Hauge Apostille Convention is a treaty signed between 120 countries. The countries who are party to this agreement will recognise each other's official documents if they are apostilled by the origin country's foreign office.

If two countries are part of the convention, then an apostille is sufficient to certify a document's validity and removes the need for double certification.

When making certain applications in another country, you may be asked to provide a legalised UK document.

The Legalisation Office will check the document, including whether the signature, stamp or seal is genuine. They'll legalise the document by attaching a stamped official certificate (an 'apostille') to it.

Be aware that any documents issued outside the UK, must be legalised in the country they were issued.

If the new export market you are targeting is part of this treaty, it will make your life much easier in terms of cost and time. In countries where there are different systems for document legalisation or if the country authorities do not accept the authenticity of your original documents, you will need to allocate additional time and money for legalisation purposes. It's important to have a realistic expectation of how long this process really takes and when 'tomorrow' really means 'sometime in the future'! In an ideal world you should talk to companies who have already gone through this process for exporting to that country, but always build in time to accommodate delays in your calculations.

Speaking from experience

In 2017, our company decided to open a liaison office in Izmir, Turkey. Izmir has four universities with large translation departments and we knew it would be an ideal place for us to draw on fresh talent to grow our company. Additionally, the Turkish Government would provide a special three year exemption from VAT and corporation tax responsibilities for foreign companies, if they complied with local requirements.

It was a big advantage that Turkey is part of the Apostille convention, which has meant that our company's official documents, such as articles of association and powers of attorney, were accepted by Turkish authorities as long as these were apostilled by the UK Foreign Office - and the same applied to the Turkish translations of the same documents. This made the application process much easier.

As a result of this facility provided, after the end of the three-year period, our company decided to establish a permanent presence in Turkey, and we set up a limited company in compliance with the Turkish company regulations.

> **Business Tip**
>
> If your target country has signed the Hauge Apostille Convention then, as long as your documents are translated, and bear the apostille stamp, they will be accepted by the country to which you'll be exporting. This will help you overcome unnecessary delays when opening bank accounts, applying to government authorities for permits, employing people or simply getting entry visas for you and your staff.

Discovering packaging requirements

I've already mentioned packaging mistakes and the likely obstacles these can create. It is essential to discover these at the information gathering stage for the shortlisted new export market. Let's not forget that we have only shortlisted the country due to its potential and this is the verification stage of the potential export market.

You will need to find out:

- Any restrictions on packaging materials e.g. recyclable materials, etc.

- Labelling information that must be displayed on packaging
- Any data that must be displayed on the shipping containers or packaging
- Whether the product will need to go through any local verification before being permitted to be sold.

This information will have a direct impact on your production plans and cost projections.

We have seen examples of hold-ups by the export department due to key information missing from labelling or documentation. Our client's shipment of heavy machinery was held up because of there was no user guide in the native language. This created a major panic for the export department as they had to pay for storage and had to rearrange shipment and the subsequent delay caused extra costs and there was a serious embarrassment factor as they could not deliver the goods as promised.

Resources for researching the packaging requirements

An established competitor's packaging is always a good place to start. This is something you should be looking at as part of your market research in any case. An established competitor's products in the target marketplace will give you lots of useful information.

Any trade contacts provided by UK embassies in the target country can provide valuable advice or point you in the right direction. In most countries this essential information may be available in English as well. It is a matter of researching the information and it's also important not to rely on just one source, particularly if your findings indicate that you need to modify your packaging.

The essential approach here is not to make assumptions in regard to labelling information, sizes and colours and base all decisions on solid verified information.

Protecting your intellectual property

Businesses spend time and money to develop their intellectual property (IP). And establishing a brand can take years of hard work. This is your company's intangible asset and, like any asset, you need to protect it. Your IP is integral to your reputation and part of how customers to come to know and trust your brand.

There are four types of intellectual property rights:

- Trademarks
- Patents
- Copyrights
- Trade secrets

Your company name, your website domain, your product names are good examples of these intangible assets. Your business has some or all these, otherwise you would not be where you are today. Developing these assets has taken years of experience working with many clients, and perfecting your model based on these experiences and overcoming setbacks.

Contrary to common belief, having a registered limited company or having a registered domain name won't protect you against a competitor using the same or a similar name in another country. The only way to protect these intangible assets is to register them in the countries where you are planning to trade.

Protecting your intellectual property should be taken very seriously and I strongly recommend that you consult experts in this subject. In this book our intention is to make sure that the IP and trademarks are your top priorities when considering global expansion.

You can take precautions to make sure that there is no danger of losing your intellectual property, so it won't be a barrier to your international trade.

There are many costly examples in the past, and these are not limited to small companies either.

In her book 'Intellectual Property Revolution' Shireen Smith states that 'The international application of IP laws is relevant to online businesses at a much earlier stage than before.

Case Study – Let culturally appropriate packaging drive your sales

A TENS (transcutaneous electrical nerve stimulation) machine is used for pain relief involving the use of a mild electrical current. The manufacturer, having successfully sold the products in the UK for many years, decided to market them in Saudi Arabia, having discovered the market potential there.

They almost went ahead with printing their current packaging in Arabic. Luckily, at this point, their advisor spotted that the appearance of the person on the packaging would not be acceptable for the Saudi market. It was fortunate for the company that they discovered the inappropriate packaging photo or product recalls would have cost them a lot of money in reprinting, repackaging and transport.

The most important tip here is that you should set all your assumptions aside when considering a new export market and base your actions on hard facts.

Discovering likely barriers for your product or service

Culture and language shape everything we do and dictate how we do it. Companies who recognise these differences enter into new markets more easily and generally avoid costly mistakes.

> ### Business Tip
>
> Pizza Hut opened its first restaurant in China in 1990 and has grown to become a leading restaurant brand with over 2200 branches in over 500 cities. Their success was based on recognising the Chinese consumer's preferences and adapting their recipes to suit local tastes.
>
> Pizza Hut carried out market research into Chinese consumer preferences, tastes and dining habits. They established that Chinese consumers do not like cheese and tomato is not a culinary ingredient in China (these are the two main pizza ingredients). Pizza Hut modified their pizza recipes, using less tomato sauce and cheese, adding locally preferred ingredients such as tuna, crab sticks, soy sauce, chicken and corn. As a result, they have continued to grow while other pizza brands lacked growth or even closed.

Understanding and respecting culture makes a big difference for any company large or small. It is key to winning customers.

What is accepted in one market is not necessarily accepted in another market.

- Mobile handsets are referred to as 'handy' in German market
- A branding company who wanted to expand their services in German speaking markets would have a rude awakening if they had not known 'brand' meant fire in German.

There are many words with totally different meanings in some languages. Even between the same language there can be colloquial differences. For instance one of the words for children in French is 'le gosse'. However in Canadian French 'le gosse' means 'testicles'.

Trolley in the UK is normally used for supermarket shopping, but in Canada and the USA it can be used to mean a tram.

The languages and culture are different for each country and can be vastly different between continents.

Countries closer to each other may share similar values cultures. These can be used as an advantage.

A Chinese company would feel a lot less foreign doing business in Far East countries than in Europe.

Most Nordic companies share similar values and cultures. For the same reason it is not a surprise that Chinese is the lingua franca in the Far East.

Language and cultural barriers are among the top barriers mentioned by the companies trading internationally or perceived to be the biggest barrier to overcome.

Top 5 takeaways about intellectual property

1. Having a registered a limited company or domain name will not protect your trademark or brand name
2. You will need to register your IP for each territory to protect them
3. You need to protect your intangible assets in the same way as your tangible assets
4. You need to make sure your existing packaging designs are suitable for the new market
5. Remember most product recalls are based on labelling mistakes.

Summary

Now you have verified your choice of new export market by getting all the data and statistics together, you should be satisfied that the chosen market is the one you would like to expand to. Now you can move to the next stage where the stakes get higher.

The Information Gathering step is crucial for understanding the market, cultural and language barriers so that you can draw a short-term and long-term strategy for succeeding in this market.

No two export markets are the same and understanding and respecting the values of the new export market can make a huge difference to your business's success.

By now you will have researched legal requirements, packaging requirements, how to protect your IP and checked that your product or service has nothing misleading or inappropriate for your target market.

Now it's time to use all this information to make things happen.

Chapter 8 Navigate the Market

The exploratory stage is now over, and you are ready to move into the pre-implementation stage. This step ensures that your roll out is a success and there are no surprises or unexpected barriers. In this chapter, we will go deeper into the specific country and set your path for success.

There is nothing better than going to the country to see the place yourself. Attend a trade mission going to the country you are targeting. Or look for joint venture opportunities with companies who share similar targets with similar synergy. Any of these activities will warm you up to the country and help to discover something about it that you did not know before.

However this stage can also be successfully completed remotely when there are travel restrictions in place.

Every country is different in how they do business, how they negotiate, and business terms and laws may be different too. It is essential that these are observed from the beginning and all necessary provisions are in place. These include fact-finding about all these issues as well as reaching agreements with local distributors and government officials, banks and currency exchange providers, storage facilities and so forth.

There will be mainly two stages here. One is to do with your product/service and the other is your localisation strategy for the new market.

Establish your targets realistically

Based on your studies it is important to have realistic and achievable targets for the new export country. You should be basing the targets on hard data and market trends. Having a contingency plan at this stage is also important in case you face any unexpected delays or come across any barriers.

As you would do in your home market, you need to carry out the sale projections and budget calculations. At the same time allowing room for errors and unexpected events in the new market are also important.

The best product/service for the new export market

You may have a range of products or services created over the years to service your domestic market. These are created to meet customer demand as well as to deliver customer satisfaction.

When you are targeting a new export market, you are starting to create a new customer journey for that market.

You may need to develop new products or amend certain products to meet the new market's demand.

The new country testing kit results will provide information about the new export market. Based on this you can review your product range and see the most suitable product for the new market.

Alternatively, to meet demand you may create new markets and join the ranks of the global brands such as KFC, Dunkin Donuts and similar.

Another aspect that needs examination is packaging. Look closely at the type of packaging provided by the competitors. It is minimalist or glossy? From this you can assess customer expectations.

To engage customers' attention, it is important to meet their expectations.

Companies with an open-minded and innovative product creation mindset are likely to excel in new markets.

Legal matters: VAT, custom duties, quotas and documentation

Quotas, customs duties and VAT regulations vary greatly from country to country and also depend on certain products and services.

Quotas

A quota is a limit to the quantity coming into a country. Countries may impose quotas on some products to protect domestic producers.

Tariffs

Tariffs or custom duties are taxes on imported goods. Tariffs are created to protect domestic industries and used by developing economies as well as advanced economies.

Quotas and tariffs are essentially barriers to international trade. Therefore you need to discover these as early as possible.

Get your documents legalised

There is a Legalisation Office in the UK that will legalise certain official UK documents. Legalisation is the official confirmation that a signature, seal or stamp on a document is genuine. You will often be required to produce official documents by the new export market's authorities. These could be a memorandum of articles, submitted company accounts, certificate of fiscal residence proving that your company is registered in the UK for tax purposes.

The Legalisation Office will check the document and legalise it by attaching a stamped official certificate called an 'apostille'.

Some of these documents might include a UK birth certificate, a marriage certificate, and company documents such as your company registration certificate.

For legalisation purposes, it's useful to find out if the country is part of the 1961 Hague Convention. There are 83 member countries, and members' authorities will accept all legal documents if these are apostilled by the UK Foreign Office.

This is an easy enough service to use and your admin team and, in some cases, your language service provider can assist you with this.

When we were setting up our liaison office in Turkey in 2018, we needed to provide Turkish authorities with various company documents in Turkish.

Turkey is part of the 1961 Hague Convention and, because all our translations were apostilled by the Legalisation Office, we did not experience any delays in setting up the liaison office.

Business Tip

To get any translated document legalised by the Legalisation Office, the translations need to be confirmed by a Notary Public or a registered solicitor in the UK.

Always check the country's specific requirements for legalisation to prevent any delays.

For example, Chinese authorities may require further authentication of the legalised documents by the Chinese Embassy. Therefore, a thorough investigation on your part is essential.

Your localisation strategy for customer engagement

Localisation is a process where a brand's identity, content, products and marketing messages are adapted for the local market to suit local customs, cultures and language conventions. Localisation does not simply mean translating texts, it may include adaptations of colour, images and design elements.

A good example of this is 'Carphone Warehouse' in the UK (who recently became part of Currys). The name 'Carphone Warehouse' which is rather outdated and irrelevant now, had been accepted by UK customers. But the same name would not be relevant in a new export market. For this reason, they were called 'Phone Warehouse' in most other countries. This was a smart adaptation by their management.

If we look at successful global brands there is one common theme between them. They may all have different journeys and sell different products or services. But the common theme between global brands such AirBnB, Uber, Netflix, McDonalds, Starbucks, Subway and many others is in their approach to local markets. All these successful brands take localisation to heart and localise for each individual market, while keeping their corporate identity.

The main purpose of your localisation strategy is to create customer satisfaction. This includes making information, user guides, marketing messages available in the native language so that customers get clear and comprehensive information about your product in your marketing, packaging and in store. Collaboration with a well-equipped and experienced translation service provider will be very useful.

Your localisation strategy should not be limited to translating existing content for the new market. Your existing content is already localised for your home market, but don't assume it will work just as well in your new market. It needs to be reviewed and made suitable for the new market.

Localising marketing content

Marketing is the way to reach customers hearts and create emotions, so it must be relevant and suitable for your target customers. There are many languages and cultures in the world. The same words can create different reactions in different cultures. For instance, different colours mean different things in different cultures. Red may mean danger or stop in the UK, but in China it indicates luck. And be careful of using green or black in China – they have negative messages.

There are over 6000 languages in the world and they can be either a low context language or a high context language. In high context languages, the way you address your ideal customer can make a huge difference.

In low context languages, such as English, the word 'you' is applicable to young, old, professional, housewife etc. In high context languages, there are different versions of 'you' and using the wrong version can easily alienate your target audience. In this respect your marketing content should be localised to create the right approach for your target audience.

Translation of user guides and data sheets are reasonably straightforward, as they contain basic information and are generally written in neutral language.

Even so, localisation of certain terms must be done so that the readers of the user guides do not get confused. Where medical devices are concerned this can literally be the difference between life and death.

Localisation is a subject in its own right. Here we are just scratching the surface. Brands who pay attention to localisation issues are usually much more successful.

Let's have a look at some examples.

Case Study – Launching in new markets the Netflix way

Netflix sets a great example on how to reach to an audience in a new market. Netflix does not take a wholesale approach, they create original content for each country as well as subtitling or dubbing in the local languages.

Their productions are designed to meet the requirement of the market's culture and language, even using local production teams and resources. This is the secret of their success.

They produced a trailer for the Turkish market for their launch in 2016, and anyone who did not know that they are a global brand, would be excused to believe that Netflix is a Turkish company. In the trailer there were Turkish actors, and the subject matter was based on an entertainment program that was popular at the time.

It comes as no surprise that Netflix is hugely popular in many countries because they manage to connect with their local audiences at every level as any other local company. In the first quarter of 2021, Netflix's revenue generated from USA & Canada was $3.17 billion and rest of the world was $3.93 billion.

They are truly a great example of acting local while being global: GLOCAL

We all recognise these brands in any country we visit, or their website in any language it is available in. The content is localised, but the corporate identity, logo, colours and the main themes are easily spotted.

GLOCAL – be local while remaining global

The term GLOCAL was coined to represent this hybrid approach and cater to a local market, while retaining a global mindset.

Global brands have resources and budgets to spend on localisation, but nobody has infinite resources. Let's not forget that these companies are accountable to their shareholders, so any spending needs to be justified and must generate income.

The purpose of this book is to help business owners to put in place structures and processes that improve their localisation workflow and investment, whatever stage they're currently at.

Localisation steps for your new export market

Attention to localisation is one the biggest differentiators for success in new markets. Localisation includes:

- Taking payment in the local currency
- Respecting the local market's habits for receiving goods (i.e. In France many customers prefer to collect from delivery points)

- Respecting language and cultural factors
- Producing content for the local market.

Preparing your website for the target country

Your website is likely to be the main source for your new customers to get information about your brand. Even if you are going through the local distributors to sell your products, it is still an important factor for brand awareness and your reputation.

Therefore, it is important to review how fit your website is for this purpose.

In preparation for website localisation you will need to decide:

- How the domains will be organised in the new languages. Will you have one top level domain with different language options or a folder structure or create sub-domains? Or will you have a separate domain name for each country?
- What are the keywords for each country – (before copywriting can start)
- What are the most suitable products for each country? Will you market all your products in all countries the same way or will some changes be needed?
- A website localisation strategy: which technology will be used for the translation process, including how to deploy product changes in price, product

descriptions or new products for the other languages? There are technologies that enable these to be updated automatically and notified to the translation platform. Otherwise any updates in the English language website will take time to implement in other languages and, of course, there will be a cost.

Now let's have a look at some options:

Landing pages for the new market

Creating landing pages in the language of the new market will allow you to target your audience.

It will also allow you to provide information in the local languages. You can capture information and track engagement using Google analytics.

Here are five reasons you need landing pages in a local language:

1. It is the quickest way to inform your customers
2. You can measure engagement in your new export market
3. It showcases your products that are intended for the new market
4. It's a cost-effective way to provide information
5. It makes it easier to generate leads in the new market.

Microsite for the new market

A microsite is an individual web page or small collection of web pages that act as a separate entity for a brand. A microsite can have its own domain or may exist as a subdomain.

Microsites can be used to help companies to:

- Highlight a specific campaign or target specific buyer personas in the new market
- Tell a short story about your brand or a product
- Invite users with a specific call-to-action
- Test engagement in the new country market
- Create another platform to gain online visibility.

Microsites can be temporary. Once a specific marketing campaign comes to an end the microsite can be taken down. However, they also can be incorporated into the main site, or continuously updated depending on the company's strategy.

What are the benefits?

- It will increase your visibility
- You can target a new export market in their native language It is affordable, as it will only need content for selected products
- It's easier to highlight a clear call to action
- It can be used to boost your SEO with links to the main website.

It will be important for you to plan your microsite strategy to get the maximum return on investment in the new export market. This should include a clear headline, good copy in the local language, paying attention to keywords and a strong call to action with clear buttons and links to your main website to improve SEO.

Your website localised into the language of the new market

This is a viable option for a long-term solution. After you have established the viability of the new market, it would make total sense to have a localised website for that market.

Companies who have taken this route, have seen increased revenue. Also, all global brands without exception provide their customers with a localised experience.

Avoid these ten website localisation mistakes

1. Failing to plan and document the localisation process. If each stage isn't taken into account as it unfolds, you will have no control over the process. Localisation should be part of your global strategy

2. Not securing top level domain names for other countries or not having a clear domain structure for the translated site, either on a language or country basis

3. Not making sure the content is in plain language and is free from culturally-biased content. Are all the pictures and colours appropriate for the target country?

4. Not checking with your web developer if the English website has multilingual support. Some website platforms may not have multilingual support or may not support certain languages, such as Arabic

5. Starting translation before doing keyword research, so the keywords don't appear in the translated text, and your website will not be found in local searches

6. No clear call to action on your pages, specific to the country. The call to action on the main website may not be relevant for the translated version

7. Not using country-specific, top-level domains, folders or not using language specific to the target country

8. Not setting Google Analytics and Google Search Console (previously Google Webmaster tools) properly to monitor traffic and highlight issues with the site that need to be addressed

9. Not making your website visible for the target country. Without taking into account keywords and TLD (top level domain) usage, your website may stay invisible for the target country or language

10. Not able to reply to a non-English enquiry.

Case Study – Persil in its many different forms

Persil is a German brand of laundry detergent manufactured and marketed by Henkel around the world except in the United Kingdom, Ireland, France, Latin America (except Mexico), China, Australia and New Zealand, where it is manufactured and marketed by Unilever.

Being part of a huge company like Henkel, Persil products have been manufactured and sold around the globe for decades by both Henkel and Unilever.

Persil brand has different names in different countries. Henkel markets Persil under the name "Dixan" in Greece, Italy and Cyprus; and under the name "Wipp" in Spain and China.

In Belgium, where both Henkel's Persil and Dixan can be found at major retailers, the Persil brand name is given priority by Henkel in its marketing. Henkel sells its Persil formulation in France under the name "Le Chat", as Unilever owns the licence to the Persil trademark in that country.

In 2008, Henkel launched Persil Abaya Shampoo, which is the equivalent of Persil Black in Saudi Arabia (the abaya is the scarf Arabic women wear over their heads to cover their hair – and it is always black).

> *Later on they introduced the product to Gulf Cooperation Council region markets as well. With its black colour-lock technology, the detergent ensures that the garment maintains its blackness, while simultaneously protecting and cleaning the fabric. Although the products look to be the same, Persil markets Abaya Shampoo as a special detergent for Abayas in the Arabic market.*
>
> *It can make a lot of sense when we think about the fact that probably one of the only black coloured clothing garments in a climate like Arabia is the abaya, so Arabic women are the perfect target audience for a dark-coloured clothing detergent.*
>
> *Persil also introduced several different fragrances of Persil Abaya over years to appearl to a wider range of customer preferences and broaden its reach.*

Packaging mistakes to avoid for the new market

Most of product recalls are due to packaging mistakes, irregularities, or not having the correct packaging information required for the new export market. Product recalls can create financial difficulties, delay getting into the market and also can kill your appetite for entering into new markets.

Finding out the necessary legal requirements for packaging information well in advance and making sure the packaging and labelling are following the local requirement can be easily achieved. This will save you a lot of time and money and will enable you to move forward seamlessly with your plans for the new country market.

Packaging plays such an important role in the consumers' purchasing decisions. For this reason, companies spend a lot of time and money to get the packaging right. Good packaging will get the customer's attention. However, unintentionally getting it wrong can result in painful consequences.

The top packaging mistakes to avoid

Colours on the packaging that clash with the local culture

Using the wrong colour for the target country can be disastrous for an otherwise good product. For example, some colours are associated with death in some cultures or certain colours may have a religious significance. Packaging colours need to be chosen carefully and should be neutral when possible, in order to keep costs down.

Choosing inappropriate photographs

Photographs can help tremendously to increase a product's appeal. However, if the photos or graphics used are not in line with the target country's traditions or consumer expectations, photos that were meant to help can be a problem for your marketing campaign. Photos and graphics need to be considered at the design stage when it is cheaper to resolve any issues that are identified.

Making the typesetting process unnecessarily complicated

It makes sense to get as many different languages as possible onto the same packaging. This will save time and money. But, different languages, particularly right-to-left languages, require different skills and resources in order to get the information right.

Using a translation company equipped with a typesetting studio can be a simple and effective solution. They can make sure that all of the languages appear correctly on your packaging.

Assuming that existing packaging will work in any country

Different countries may have different packaging requirements and restrictions. Therefore, packaging designed for your domestic market that complies with the local regulations may require modification for other countries.

The relative costs and time required to do this needs to be considered at the planning stage. Failing to conform to the target country's regulations may result in delays and, in some cases, in product recalls.

Not briefing your designer about your international marketing plans

If your designer is not aware of your overseas requirements, they will not design the original artwork with an international mindset. Text that is integrated into graphics will mean extra cost and time as the graphic needs to be localised for each language.

For example, avoid text going over double page spreads or complex graphic shapes with text running around them. This will make right-to-left language formatting, such as Arabic and Hebrew, much easier since the direction of pages must be mirrored for these languages.

Not allowing enough space for other languages

Text for some languages will take up more space than English text. For example, a German translation will contain approximately 20% more characters than English. If there is not enough space, then a small size type may have to be used, or the design may need to be modified.

Using product names with adverse meanings in other languages

A global brand name check should be the first step before deciding on the product name and packaging slogan. Make sure that the brand name and product taglines do not have any adverse meanings in different languages.

Case Study – Exporting fine wine to China

China is known to be a growing market for fine wine producers. Like most food and beverage consumables there are some strict regulations in place for fine wine too.

For example, Chinese customs will keep any imported fine wines in storage for three weeks before clearing them for distribution.

During this time there needs to be special storage facilities for the wine, and this requires planning as well as budgeting for the extra cost.

If the wine were to be kept in unsuitable storage, the quality may be adversely affected and the wine will lose its value or possibly go to waste.

You must study the regulations and local standards in advance before you start exporting food and beverage consumables into China as there are strict regulations and they quickly change as well.

Top 5 takeaways

1. This stage can be completed remotely if there are travel restrictions

2. This is the stage where you establish connections with your target market

3. Tackle all legal matters such as VAT, tariffs and quotas

4. Your localisation strategy for your website and marketing documents are in place to reach your target customers

5. Your packaging and labelling are fully in compliance with the local market.

Summary

In this chapter Navigate the Market you have explored the pre-implementation stage. Because the next step is the roll out step where everything will come together.

At the end of this step, you will have gathered all necessary market data as well as legal information to get started.

You are now equipped with all market specific information and ready to roll out to your next export market.

- You have chosen a suitable export strategy
- You have completed or put in place your product packaging plan
- You have decided on your localisation strategy.

Now you are ready and cannot wait to get started – it's time to go into action.

Chapter 9 Go Operational

This chapter covers the implementation stage. You will complete your research into potential export markets, so you have the information that will ensure your decision is based on facts, not guesswork. You have chosen your first market and your product or service is ready for delivery. Now you've built a strong foundation you're ready to go into action.

You have the products required in the new export market; you have systems in place to conduct the new business venture. Your business will flourish further by expanding into the new market and continue to grow, which in turn, will help you create new products and conquer new markets.

The essence of this stage is to do it in a timely and well-orchestrated way. Unnecessary delays at this stage can result in losing your competitive advantage and can result in losing your potential market share.

This is the stage where you double-check everything to make sure no critical step has been missed before you roll out.

It's time to launch your operations in the new export market.

The 15-step final roll-out checklist

Whether you are an e-commerce business, marketing digital products or sending physical goods to a new market, this is a new beginning for you. Get this started correctly and you will have potential new markets for growth and new doors will be opened for you. This is much more doable and cost-effective than trying to grow in a saturated market or where you have diminishing returns.

This new market presents you with an opportunity to get connected with a new audience and once this is successful, you can repeat the process for other export markets.

Being involved in international trade will also increase your company's innovative and creative skills, which will help you offer even better products or services to your domestic market.

It is critical that you have the right start in the new export market. Here is a 15-step checklist that may be useful for you to check against your progress. The checklist is in the resources for you to download so you can check you've completed every step and work on any weak links.

1. You shortlisted a new export market(s) by completing the New Export Market Toolkit

2. Your completed brand name checklist to make sure your brand name is suitable for the target market

3. Your product is suitable for the new export market

4. You have adapted or checked your product for the new export market

5. You have decided on your export strategy for the new export market

6. You have sales projections and budgets in place for the next 12 months

7. You are aware of packaging and labelling requirements for the new export market

8. You have acquired all necessary export documentation

9. You checked if any documents need to be legalised

10. You have created a communication plan for customer engagement

11. You have a localisation strategy for your website, marketing materials and product information sheets

12. You have established contacts on the ground

13. You are aware of VAT and other tax-related regulations of the new market

14. Your checked that your product is not restricted by any quotas or tariffs

15. You can receive payments in the local currency and are aware of the preferred payment methods of the new market.

You can download this checklist from ttcwetranslate.com/ book/checklists

Let's look at some of the strategies that can make a difference to your success.

Your business card – the most cost-effective icebreaker

Should you have your business card in the local language? In many countries people do not often understand some of job titles such as CTO, CFO, CEO, MD, CMO. If you have one of these titles, and your counterpart does not get your job function, you may not get their interest to start with. After all, you are more likely to get the attention of people with a similar ranking as yourself, which opens the door for some serious talks.

It's not about saving money as a business card, in say Chinese, would probably be the smallest item compared to flights, hotel costs, exhibition fees and other preparations. That one item makes it clear to your potential customer who you are, your job title (very important for high context cultures), what your business does, and demonstrates you're serious about doing business. In other words, it's a highly cost-effective ice breaker.

I wonder how many potentially important conversations have not even got started because the person you try to introduce yourself to did not understand your job title and thought 'why should I speak with this person'?

Alternatives if you are unable to travel

If you are motivated by being actually present and experiencing the new export market or you want to see the first experience of your customers getting your products or using them, travel restrictions may create problems for you.

In 2021 there have been many travel restrictions and some countries, such as China, are not allowing visitors into the country. When there is no definite timeline for lifting these restrictions, it is important that you think of some alternatives to travelling. This will ensure that your investment does not go to waste.

I can appreciate the importance of seeing your goods on display or an opportunity to engage with customers. While online meetings, video calls with potential customers or business partners are no direct replacement, they will get the job done.

Here are some tips for online meetings that I've gathered through years of working with providers and customers from many different cultures.

- Discover your contact's preferred platform. Is it Zoom, Skype, Google Meet, Microsoft Teams or something else?
- You may be at home, but this is a business meeting. Dress suitably and moderately
- Make sure there is good lighting in the room and that your face is well-lit. Avoid appearing as a back-lit silhouette. A halo lamp or other diffused light costs very little
- Check that what will appear on your screen behind you reflects a business environment. There have been some widely publicised instances of unexpected and inappropriate items appearing on bookshelves behind a participant on a video call
- Speak slowly and make sure they you voice is heard at the other side
- There may be awkward silences or interruptions by your counterpart. Do not take this the wrong way. Depending on the culture of the person you are engaging with, both can be perfectly normal for the other culture

- Pay attention to gender issues. It may be wise to include a male colleague in the meeting if you are a female executive or the other way round to make the other participants feel comfortable
- Ask questions if anything is not clear, and do not be offended if they ask you direct questions
- Confirm the key points of the meeting in writing to make sure there are no misunderstandings
- If you plan to record the meeting ensure everyone involved is aware of this and make the recording available to them later.

How to create engagement in your new export market

Creating engagement in the early stages of your roll out is essential to a successful launch. Whether you have business-to-business customers or are selling directly to consumers, mobilising your resources to create engagement with them at the beginning will increase the success of your launch. This means you can leverage your advantage of being the new product on the market, which will get more attention.

Consider the following:

- Define what good engagement means for your operations in the new market. i.e., this can be simply the opening rates of your mail out, or replies you receive following a campaign or number of quote requests you receive

- What can you do to create engagement?
- How can you measure the engagement created?

Putting in place these steps will help you to assess the engagement you have with your target audience objectively.

Brand awareness in the new market

You are by now aware of the new export market's social media preferences and which platforms are popular. These are cost-effective strategies aimed at raising brand awareness for your product:

- Consider running weekly Facebook competitions to raise brand awareness and to create engagement
- Facebook adverts to enable you to target the audience that matches your ideal customer.
- Create a poll or survey to get feedback
- Share a series of videos and blogs across social media platforms
- Get your customers to share their experiences on social media and find a way to reward them with something that is low cost, but high value.

These activities require a sustained effort from your marketing team, ideally working with local content creators. It is critical that you consult local content creators for guidance and suitability, while keeping all content consistent with your corporate brand guidelines. This will avoid any unwitting gaffs that may alienate your potential customers.

A 'must have' – your corporate brand guidelines

This is one document that is a 'must have' when you have content created by multiple sources. A typical brand guideline provides information such as:

- Your corporate colour references with PMS, CMYK, RGB and Hex specifications

- Your corporate logo. Where is it available to download in different formats (eps, png, jpg) and how it should be used as well as how it must not be used

- Your corporate typography details; font styles, point sizes and where to download the fonts from if they are custom made or part of a paid library

- Imagery to be used and how to access the image library. Also the company policy about the strict use of approved and licensed materials in order to prevent any copyright breaches

- Examples of your company tone of voice: friendly, professional, chatty

- Your tone of voice for the new export market. This is important for high-context cultures where the form of address changes depending on the age, profession, and social position and is something you will need to discuss and agree before the launch.

Over the years I have come across many examples of poor use of corporate logos and typefaces and even brand names appearing differently in different countries. It seems like each country's branch see themselves as independent from the main brand. It's essential that you provide brand and style guidelines for your company.

If you do not currently have brand guidelines, this is an excellent time to create them. This document should be made available to all departments involved in creating content and any advertising or marketing agencies you work with. This will ensure a consistent corporate style that will inspire customer confidence in every country in which you operate.

Branding is easy to get wrong

During a meeting of an international company with a presence in over 15 countries, the global CEO collected business cards from colleagues who worked in several different countries.

When he laid the business cards on a desk side-by-side, it looked like the business cards were from 15 different companies even though all the people worked for the same company.

It only takes small details to alter the brand image; use of a different typecase, the logo placed in different places or in a different size, and colour variations because company's correct brand colours have not been used.

As a result, every country branch was instructed to get their business cards reprinted following strict corporate guidelines.

Advertising and promotions in the new market

Brand awareness is important in any market. In a global world, brand awareness and brand consistency go hand-in-hand. The biggest global brands are successful because they have systems in place to ensure brand consistency and leverage their global reputation in every new country.

As a small or medium-sized company executive, you can use this to your advantage. Your consistent and regular brand awareness activities will directly affect your brand awareness in the new export market.

Nowadays it is usual to come across product reviews in other languages in Amazon listings. If I am looking to buy a product, I am interested in any review regardless of the country it comes from and I found it reassuring that there are reviews from international customers.

How to leverage your brand image worldwide

You represent your company and your image and reputation as an executive can support the brand's image in the new country.

When customers know and trust the company executives, they have no problem trusting the brand. A good example of this is Tesla cars.

Even though Tesla has been in production for less time than other known car brands, it is globally respected because everyone knows Elon Musk from his high profile activities well-reported in the media.

Elon Musk's reputation is aligned with Tesla and they have no problem selling their cars despite overall diminishing car sales due to the COVID-19 pandemic.

Faceless companies vs high profile founders

A company with a 'face', an entrepreneur who steps up to represent the company, adds another layer to brand awareness. It will be impossible to match Elon Musk's impact, but you don't need this sort of impact.

If you are entering into a new export market, where your brand is not known, then this strategy of 'company with a face' will be relevant for you. Today we are living in a global village, thanks to the platforms such as Facebook and LinkedIn.

In any advertising strategy it's good practice to include a range of online tactics to get exposure and reputation for the brand.

Getting your profile or an interview in the relevant press in your new export market can make a big difference to the perception of your brand.

Think of the success of brands like Virgin (Richard Branson), Microsoft (Bill Gates), Remington (Victor Kiam - 'I liked it so much I bought the company').

You don't have to have such a high profile, but people 'buy' people and knowing who is the guiding force behind an organisation helps people to trust the products.

This is equally important for forming joint venture partnerships. Particularly in high context cultures, the face of the company can make such a big difference.

This brings us to the next important factor for your success in the new market; forming joint ventures with like-minded companies who have non-competing products.

Forming joint ventures

When you connect with a like-minded company in the new market and form a joint-venture or trading agreement things will have a different - and positive - perspective. The earlier you establish this, the better your launch into a new market will be.

Joint venture partnerships can cover a wide range of subjects: your distributor or export management company or a company with a complementary product would be an ideal JV partner.

Primarily, when you have a joint venture partner on the ground, you are no longer a newcomer to the market. You are no longer a brand trying to enter a foreign market. You have aligned your brand with a local company or brand and now can enjoy the facilities they can provide for you.

JV partnerships are clearly important and can help you tremendously at the beginning of your journey in the new market. But should they be formed at any cost? Absolutely not. What criteria can you use for forming such partnerships?

It should be clear to all of us by now that we live in a global village and what happens in any one place can have effects in other parts of the world. This is something we would use to our advantage as a reputable company working with principles.

In this respect your company's core values should be the guiding criteria for forming such strategic partnerships.

When you share the same or similar core values with another company, it will be so much easier to agree the details on such matters as customer care, working with integrity, processes and systems, use of social media and many other aspects that impact on your brand and image.

If your core values are based on customer care and investing in your team, then it is unlikely that you will have a long-term partnership with a company who only focus on making profits and everything else comes second or third.

In such cases avoiding these companies may be hard to do at the beginning, but will save you harder and probably costly decisions in the future.

Your core values should be your guiding principles for forming JVs as well as hiring local employees. Having team members who do not share your company's core values will create barriers in the future.

Case Study – Why it took Starbucks 47 years to enter the Italian market

Starbucks is in 78 countries and has over 28,000 locations in the world. But they didn't manage to open their first coffee store in Italy until September 2018, as the Italian market has been one of the hardest to conquer.

Italy is Europe's second largest importer of coffee beans and it accounts for 14% of European coffee consumption.

In order to investigate the reasons, we need to look at some historical facts. Italy is the country that created the cappuccino in the 18th century. This drink was unknown outside Italy until the 1930s, but it is now one of the most popular coffee drinks in the world.

Italy's coffee shop culture is quite different to the one enjoyed in the UK. Italians get their coffees in coffee bars and, generally, do not stay there for too long. Independent cafes have 90% of the market; global brands have a much smaller share.

After many years of trying, Starbucks opened its first shop in 2018 in Milan. This was only possible after Starbucks had understood the new market.

They realised that Italian coffee culture is very different from other countries. Starbucks had to align itself with the local economy.

They offered locally roasted coffee by forging partnerships with the famous bakery, Princi, in which Starbucks became an investor and global licensee in 2016.

They chose Milan, business capital of Italy, for their first branch. The building used to be the city's historic post office, with traditional-style marble floors and a huge in-house coffee roaster.

Starbucks now has 11 stores in Italy. This is still far away from the 536 stores they have in Turkey and 187 in France, but going in the right direction.

What can you learn from Starbucks's experience? They could only succeed in Italy after they recognised the cultural differences and decided to develop market entry strategies for the Italian market. As a result of their relationship with Princi, Starbucks started rolling our Princi products in their chosen global locations.

Don't take your eye off the ball

It is easy to be distracted by your other operations particularly if you are based in your home country. This could mean you are inclined to spend more time on your domestic market. However, your export markets need the same attention as your home market, initially even more.

You need to check and assess your marketing and sales activities monthly and quarterly. In order to raise your brand awareness in your new market, you need your marketing to work beautifully and within budget.

Ideally you will have targets in terms of acquiring customers, number of visitors to your website, or webstore and the number of enquiries you need to receive to meet your sales targets.

Ongoing comparison of the actual figures to the budgetary ones will help you to evaluate how your business is doing in the new market.

Top 5 takeaways

1. You ticked all boxes in the final fifteen step checklist

2. You have not overlooked an ice-breaker to make a memorable first impression

3. Your brand guidelines will help you establish your brand consistently in the new market

4. You are aware of local culture and willing to align your positioning accordingly

5. You have plans in place for promotions and for forming joint ventures.

Summary

In this chapter you have covered all the aspects of going operational in the new export market. The 15-step checklist will ensure you are on the right track. Tips on meeting remotely as an alternatives to travelling to your chosen country, will help to work around any travel restrictions you may face.

Now it's time to learn from major global brands and how you can use some of their strategies to your advantage.

The means of creating engagement with your new customer base and the main strategies for this important activity, with your online tactics, are all planned out. You've explored joint venture options in the new market and already shortlisted strategic partners for this.

Now you are operational in your selected new export market. The ongoing review of your company's operations and sales is critical for your success in this new market.

It is important to make sure your new market meets your expectations.

Chapter 10 Open for Business

In today's globalised economy, growing globally is no longer a luxury for SME executives, it's a necessity. These are challenging, uncertain times for businesses everywhere. In 2020, the COVID-19 pandemic wrought total devastation on the world economy. However, companies operating globally were less affected than those who were only trading in their domestic markets.

According to research by McKinsey, growth matters more than ever during challenging times. The study says that 'opportunities will not always come in traditional or even familiar locales; indeed, from 2010 to 2025, almost 50 percent of global GDP growth will take place in approximately 440 small- and medium-size cities in emerging markets.' That is real food for thought and underlines the importance of expanding globally rather than relying on a single market.

You are now operational and have put in place KPIs for assessing performance and monitoring the market for any unexpected developments and you know how to continue with innovation for your new market.

This step is about managing ongoing operations, dealing with changes in circumstances, and measuring return on investment. All your activities will be aimed at continuing to serve the new market to delight customers and create a loyal customer base.

There are many valuable lessons to be learned from global brands so you avoid expensive mistakes.

Develop a product innovation mindset

This is by far the most important aspect of any business. It keeps your business on the path towards growth as well as providing solutions for your customers. Customer requirements change over the years and it is important to respond to these changes. Sometimes the product you have developed may have cost a lot of both time and money, but if it becomes obsolete due to changes in consumer behaviour or technological advancements, then it is important to replace it with a product that is in demand.

One important aspect of product innovation is that it is driven by the company's management. That means the innovation mindset starts with you. The UK government offers generous research and development grants, and it will pay for you find out what is available that is suitable for your business.

Innovate for the local market

Initially, innovation will take most of your team's time and energy. It is important to get this right and monitor progress in the new market. However, this is not a one-off, even after you've introduced your product to the new market, it is important to maintain the same level of awareness of market demands. It is like making a new friend; you both discover new things about each other as time goes by.

Once you have completed the initial stage, you will start discovering different aspects of the new market and start getting to know it better. It will be a market where you want to delight your customers. This will lead to new stages of product development and innovation for your newly-found market.

Small to medium-sized companies are better placed to innovate products for their new markets than large multinational corporations. They can respond quickly unlike the larger companies who have layers of management and committees to approve any new products.

However there are exceptions to this and Dometic, a Swedish outdoor living company, is a prime example of how innovations can continue in large companies and how these will shape the future of the company.

Dometic case study – from inventing refrigeration to becoming a global mobile living giant

Website: https://www.dometic.com/en

Dometic manufactures a variety of mobile living products, most notably coolers, water heaters, energy and safety solutions for caravans, RVs, pleasure boats etc. They operate in about 100 countries and the Dometic Group turnover in 2019 was USD 2.2 billion.

Dometic's roots go back to two young Swedish engineers who invented the technology that allowed commercial production of refrigerators 100 years ago. This is considered by some to be one of the ten most important innovations of the past century. They were acquired by Electrolux in 1925 and their business was mainly in the US for this reason.

From 2001 Dometic became independent and decided to forge their own path. They noticed that more and more people around the world want a mobile lifestyle. Whether for leisure or work, they share some common needs like hygiene, cooking, heating and so on. This became Dometic's foundation and they adapted a new concept: "Mobile living made easy".

In this regard Dometic is not an ordinary large company. Dometic sets an example of how a large company can continue with innovation and develop a global mindset.

Monitor progress and measure ROI

Operating in an export market is bit like a football team playing an away game. The team is not familiar with the grounds and missing their usual army of supporters.

Even if it feels like this for you, the sooner you get to know the new market the better it will be for your business. You will need good and complete information to monitor the progress of your business. Otherwise, you may misinterpret a drop in sales or in customer engagement. This is particularly important if you are selling directly to consumers.

For instance, in France, it is common for most people to take their annual summer holidays at very similar times. This may directly affect your business both for sales and employees, particularly if you are employing local staff. However, if you are aware of this, you can plan ahead and adjust your projections accordingly.

Future-proof your business in the new market

Without doubt, the hardest part is to get started in a new export market. Once you are up and running, it is important to continue with the journey and get a strong foothold in the new market. This will safeguard your initial investment as well as continuing your growth.

There may be unexpected events that will take place in the future, which are beyond your control. But you need to do everything possible to future–proof your business. The best way to do that is to aim to exceed your customers' expectation and accept nothing less from your team.

Aiming to delight your customers means you follow the buying trends in the new market, monitor any complaints and have a prompt and positive response. This will ensure you relate to your customers at every level and will be aware of new trends or changes in customer behaviour.

Nestle's operations in Japan set an excellent example in how a large company should respond to a local market and how innovations can play a major part in growth. We will investigate how Nestle conquered the Japanese market with Nescafe and KitKat.

Case Study - How Nestle conquered the Japanese Market with Nescafe and KitKat

Nestle is the world's biggest food company with a turnover of USD 93 billion. They wanted to grow their business in Japan as it is one of the largest economies in the world.

Unhappy with their low returns in Japan with Nescafe, Nestle executives adopted a different strategy for the tea loving Japanese market. As a result, today Japan is one of world's biggest coffee importers and, not surprisingly, Nestle is the market leader there.

In the 1970s Nestle carried out research and discovered that tea has a strong emotional imprint with Japanese people, whereas coffee was not part of the Japanese culture with a very superficial demand.

This led Nestle to add coffee flavour to sweets, creating a taste for coffee that they did not previously had. Nestle started making caffeine-free coffee flavoured desserts for kids too.

Nestle continued to innovate and created products suitable for the Japanese market.

1. Nescafe Ambassador: In 2012 Nestle launched the ambassador programme to designate a person in a

workplace as 'office barista'. Nestle provided ambassadors with subsidised coffee machines and Nescafe became synonymous with work breaks where colleagues chatted and had a good time

2. *Technology: Nestle started using a robot called Pepper in 2014 to sell coffee machines in appliance stores. This worked well in the highly automated Japanese marketplace, where there is a vending machine for almost everything*

3. *Sleep Cafes: Nestle opened a sleep café in 2019 in Tokyo where people could nap and drink coffee.*

Nestle's success was not limited to Nescafe. They made an even bigger impact by developing their KitKat chocolate bars to suit the Japanese consumer.

KitKat's success in Japan

With growing Japanese interest in western culture, Nestle introduced KitKat to Japan with a distinct advantage.

KitKat was transliterated into 'Kitto Katto' which phonetically is similar to 'kitto katsu'. 'Kitto katsu' has several meanings such as 'never fail' and 'you will surely win'.

Today Nestle, with over 300 flavours, has embedded itself in the Japanese culture.

Nestle executives noticed that sales would increase of Kitto Katto every January. This was because many students take exams at this time and their parents give them KitKats as good luck presents.

It's common to wish a student taking an exam: 'kitto katsu' or 'you will win'. And the similarity with Nestle's 'Kitto Katto' makes it an easy choice to give KitKats as good luck presents.

Nestle noticed another Japanese custom in the early 2000s. Many Japanese travelling domestically, love giving regional products as gifts. Nestle began creating a range of flavours with a strong emphasis on region-specific Kitto Katto flavours. Creating flavours available only in a specific region for a limited time has become an attraction for people to visit these regions.

Some of the regional flavours are below:

Nagano – Shinshu apple Kitto Katto

Shizuoka – Wasabi Kitto Katto

Kyoto – Roasted green tea Kitto Katto

Hokkaido – Melon with mascarpone cheese Kitto Katto.

This type of innovative approach, focused on the local markets, has made a huge difference for Nestle. It is remarkable that a global company was able to have a laser-sharp focus for the Japanese market.

How can you adopt a similar approach to your products or service? What adaptations can you do to improve your customers' experience?

It all depends on the customer engagement you have in this market. Therefore, it is important to monitor the engagement you create.

Measure the effectiveness of customer engagement

It is very important that you do not assume customers are engaged just because you are publishing content. It is critical that you put in place KPIs for measuring the effectiveness of engagement and it should be done on a regular basis using a documented structure.

Here are some criteria you can use for measurement:

- The number of new orders you need on a monthly basis, e.g. 100

- Number of quotes you need to provide to achieve 100 monthly sales based on your conversion rate, e.g. a conversion rate of 40% means you need to give 250 quotes

- The number of leads you need to generate 250 quotes. E.g. if you receive 100 enquiries, but only 25 of these ask for quotes, then your conversion rate is 25% you need 1000 enquiries to generate 250 quotes.

You can fuel your global growth

It hardly needs to be said that global brands are not established overnight. Expanding globally takes time, knowledge, resources, and money. It also takes a certain mindset, strategy, and a systematic set of activities. Becoming a major global brand is harder.

Still, but, while you may not aspire to be the next Disney or Coca-Cola, those brands that have mastered the art of international trade have a lot to teach us.

You can learn a huge amount by studying what those brands have done; the tactics and approaches they have deployed and the systems they have in place. I believe you can replicate this mindset and adopt similar habits to accelerate your global growth and make international trade a reality.

Of course, most small businesses don't have a fraction of the resources of a big multi-national, but the good news is – you don't have to. Much of the research and trial and error has already been done in those high-powered boardrooms.

In Chapter 4, there are 'Five habits of global Brands worth adapting'. You can fuel your own global growth by studying the systems global brands have deployed, the approaches they have adopted and the tactics they have used.

Be growth orientated from the start

Growth is planned and executed systematically, and this is a common trait all major global brands exhibit. Examples include Uber, Airbnb, Samsung and Apple. They are very different businesses, in different sectors and with different client bases, but there is a common thread when it comes to growth orientation. It's important to embed this mindset into your business culture from day one.

Develop a global mindset with your team

We all know that the world is becoming smaller and more connected each day. There are many opportunities for companies to expand internationally, but it's important to understand why this can be beneficial before embarking on such a venture.

Nowhere is too far and no one is unreachable anymore. Global brands see the world as a connected, expansive marketplace. Developing this mindset in your team and making it part of your corporate culture will help your brand go global more easily and much quicker.

Recognise and respect different cultures

Cultural differences are often difficult to understand, but they can also be a source of strength. Recognising and respecting culture of your target audience is the only way for you to connect with them. Develop a company culture that does not make assumptions about your target market's choices. You can show your respect by celebrating the national holidays of your target market.

Make your customers' life easier

Making your customers' life easier will help them to reach a decision quicker. In order to do this, they need to be able to navigate your website easily and get your product or service information clearly.

If you provide information in their native language, enable them to make payments in their local currency and access their preferred payment options, you'll keep your customers happy. A properly localised website will help them find what they want quickly and lead to make a purchase.

Create products for local markets

Even though we live in a globalised world, customers' requirements change from country to country. A company selling baby food in the UK may use ingredients that are suitable for the UK market. If they want to sell this in another country, say China, they need to use locally grown vegetables that appeal to their preferences to attract Chinese parents' attention.

Developing products to suit local customers and preferences are vital for your global growth.

I believe that you can fuel your growth by integrating these strategies into your corporate culture.

Case Study – Gymshark - E-commerce success story

Website: https://uk.gymshark.com/

Gymshark is the UK's latest unicorn, valued at £1 bn. Founded by teenager Ben Frances in 2012 based in his mum's garage, Gymshark is selling affordable gym clothing globally.

The company's 2020 accounts show their turnover to be £260,674 million, a significant growth from 2018 when it was under £50 million. They sell directly to consumers worldwide. They have over 5 million Instagram followers.

Consulting company McKinsey has reported that due to the pandemic many consumers working from home are looking to improve their fitness, the case for home fitness, personal health and the wellbeing industry will continue growing.

Gymshark is a great example of a large company building social capital and reflecting this on their growth.

Are you ready to boost your international trade?

Now that you are in the new export market, operating successfully and turning into a profitable entity is particularly important for your company. Because your next actions will probably be based on your company's performance in this market. It is easy to continue from success in one market to add new export markets, by replicating your steps.

If you are already operating in multiple export markets and you have a profitable new market, you can easily adapt the lessons learned or new steps you have taken.

It is proven that companies increase their innovation and creativity by operating internationally. So, you can easily benefit from establishing best practice in your new market and applying it to the markets you already operate in to improve them further.

Now that you've got started in the new export market, you have successfully completed the biggest step by far. Now let's have a look at the main areas which will require continuous monitoring.

Getting these right all the time will make a significant difference in your company's future success in this new market.

Marketing

Marketing is what gets customers to the door, and it is essential for any business.

- Is your marketing working in the new market?
- What metrics are in place to measure its effectiveness?
- Are you able to create content locally or do you still leverage content from your main source language (i.e., English)?

Review your marketing strategy regularly to make sure that you are on top of trends and needs.

Communication

It's important to communicate with your local audience. Is your communication tuned into the new market's customs and culture? The sooner your team master this,the better results it will produce for you in ongoing sales.

Your product/service

Ask the question 'is our product serving the needs of the new market' and make changes if necessary. Companies who take the approach 'if it is good for our home market, it will be good for the new market' often don't monitor customer experience. Being disconnected from the customers in that market is likely to be reflected in the sales figures.

Your team

It is important that your team on the ground is in tune with the new market. This means that the local organisation must be able to make decisions. When local teams are managed by remote executives, most of the communication will be hampered by cumbersome reporting. An endless need for ongoing, detailed reports can often be seen as chore and doesn't help the ability to respond to local demands proactively.

You are more likely to experience success in the new market if you get new talent on the ground, train and nourish them and give them freedom to make decisions.

Attracting, developing, and retaining talent in the new export markets is a crucial element of your success in these markets. It will also have an impact on your customer's perception of your organisation.

Market research

You should continue with your market research activity even after getting started in the new market. Market dynamics and consumer habits can change in short space of time. It is important that you are on top of this all the time.

It took radio thirty-eight years to reach fifty million listeners. For TV to reach fifty million owners this time was 13 years. When China's Tencent developed WeChat, the mobile messaging service, it reached 300 million users in two years. This is bigger than the population of the USA.

Technologies and new habits are being adopted a lot faster than ever before and this can have an effect on any size of business. That's why staying in tune with your new market's tendencies should one of your top priorities.

Finance

Financial management is now even more important as you have expanded further afield. Managing cash-flow, organising operations, and making sure that your business will not run out of money halfway through all need attention. In order to achieve your goals you need to plan and review your finances.

Top 5 takeaways

1. Developing products for the new market should be an ongoing process

2. Finding, developing, and training local talent is a must for continued success

3. Staying in-tune with the customers is the key to success in the new market

4. Monitor current sales, but ultimately think of ways to future-proof your business

5. Develop and nurture an innovative mindset regardless of your company size.

Summary

As a result of all your preparations and the strategies you have put in place, you should be fully operational and working seamlessly towards your targets in your new market.

At this stage you have your KPIs in place and are monitoring performance to ensure you're ready if any unexpected circumstances arise.

You will keep your finger on the pulse of your new market to ensure you continue to exceed your customers' expectations and to remain responsive to their wants and needs.

Conclusion

The world has become a much smaller place due to ease of travel and modern technology. From a small company selling online to a large brand the biggest challenge is still reaching customers. For many, growing to become a large company is an impossible dream, but for a few it can be a reality. From the examples around us the biggest factor for success and a means of future-proofing a business seems to be successfully going global.

The lessons of the last decade have shown us that:

- Selling globally is a viable way to future-proof your business
- Selling globally is no longer limited to large organisations with huge budgets
- Global growth requires a global mindset
- You can learn from the experiences of existing global brands
- Customers adapt to new changes at record speed.

The success stories featured in this book show that global success requires a systematic approach, dedication to growth and, perhaps, some luck helps too.

But the single thing that seems to make the biggest difference is taking international trade seriously and following a methodology. LINGO's simple, 5-step model is intended to provide this structure, so you can turn your going global dream into a reality.

Next steps

Register your book and get on my VIP list. You will receive:

- Any updates or new checklists mentioned in the book
- Future bonuses
- Invitations to free webinars

Register your book at:
ttcwetranslate.com/registermybook/

Get your assessment

If you're ready to boost your international trade, you can get an assessment of your ability to grow globally or boost your international trade

Our new scorecard has 15 questions, covering marketing, product and market research.

You can complete this online and you will get a personalised report on the 3 key areas and how you can improve them.

It is a great complimentary tool to learn about your weakness and strengths.

To take the International Trade Scorecard visit https://global.scoreapp.com/

Book a call with me

Book a discovery call with me, where we will discuss the outcome of your scorecard (if you have taken one) and look at where you are in your global journey. Link: https://calendly.com/levent-ttc

Book me as a speaker

You can book me as a speaker for your online or live event. Please email levent@ttcwetranslate.com to receive my speaker kit.

Speaking topics include:

- Cultural differences and why you need to be aware of them for your business
- 5 Habits of major global brands and how to apply them to your business
- How to use 5 Step LINGO model for your brand
- Conquer new markets by breaking language barriers
- 5 Reasons why growing globally is relevant

Subscribe to my podcast

In my podcast 'Conquer New Markets' I interview entrepreneurs, executives and authors sharing their experiences and global journeys. It is available in all popular podcast platforms. Simply search for 'Conquer New Markets'.

If you would like to appear as my podcast guest, please email my team at admin@ttcwetranslate.com for further details.

References

'The Wealth of Nations' by Adam Smith (first published in 1776)

'Intellectual Property Revolution' by Shireen Smith (Rethink Press, 2012)

'No Ordinary Disruption' by Richard Dobbs, James Manyika and Jonathan Woetzel (PublicAffairs, 2016)

Useful books

'Kiss, Bow or Shake Hands' by Terri Morrison and Wayne A. Conaway (Adams Media, 2006)

'Riding the Waves of Culture' by Fons Trompenaars and Charles Hampden-Turner (First published by Nicholas Brealey Publishing, 1997)

'Doing Business Internationally' by Danielle Walker, Thomas Walker and Joerg Schmitz (McGraw-Hill, 2003)

'Export and Import' by Leif Holmwall (Export Pro Inc, 2016)

'Import/Export Kit for Dummies' by John Capela (John Wiley & Sons, 2016)

Links

You can access the resources mentioned in each chapter by visiting: ttcwetranslate.com/book/links

Acknowledgements

I had been working on this book since 2018, but without the contribution of the following people it would not have been possible, my sincere thanks to goes out to:

My editor, Lesley Morrisey for her navigational skills and editorial guidance. Lucy McCarraher and Joe Gregory of Rethink Press who helped bring this book into existence.

My beta readers Zeynep Turudi, Giovanni Baccini, Firat Yildizgoren and Lesley Batchelor, for taking time out from their busy schedules, their feedback has been invaluable helping me perfect the content of this book.

To my colleagues, who stepped up their efforts so that I could continue my writing without interruption. In particular, Abi Hatter, for taking on the responsibility as acting Managing Director without hesitation and Denise Robinson, for typesetting and making many suggestions along the way.

I would also like to extend my gratitude to all our clients, whose continued trust and support for us over the years, has made us the company we are today.

Finally, I want to thank my wife and my co-founder Banu Yildizgoren, together we have built a thriving business, which we are extremely proud of. I would not have been able to write this book without her help and encouragement.

The Author

It seems a long time ago when I joined the working world as a camera operator for a printing company. I spent 15 years working my way around the business as production manager, then studio manager for pre-press graphic production. This experience came in useful later.

In 1992 I co-founded TTC wetranslate Ltd, with my wife Banu and nearly three decades later, I'm proud to be in charge of a multi-award winning translation and localisation company.

I'm fortunate to have a strong team and, having qualified myself as a PRINCE2 project manager, all my key project managers also have this qualification.

In December 2009 I had a potentially life-changing accident that seriously restricted my mobility for a year. This enforced period of retrospection opened another door for me and my focus moved towards helping and supporting others both in my local community and in my industry.

I enjoy mentoring people at various stages of their journey and am honoured to be a visiting lecturer at the University of Essex.

Under TTC wetranslate's umbrella we worked with three different universities in the UK and in Turkey to create the Translation Challenge, which has now been running annually since 2013. The Challenge provides translation students with the opportunity to take part in real-life projects doing commercial translations. From the amazing feedback we get, this has made a huge impact on hundreds of students giving them a taste of what it is like to work as a professional translator.

Along with my team we have supported charities either through our own fundraising events or by participating in events organised to support a specific charity or cause. We even had team members running in a race simultaneously in the UK, Turkey and Australia!

More recently I launched a podcast channel called 'Conquer New Markets'. Over the episodes I've interviewed many successful business executives and published authors on going global, business growth and cultural matters. Perhaps you'll listen to some of the episodes on your podcast stream and, when you've put what you've learned from this book into action, maybe I'll get to interview you too one day!

List of currencies of the major trading countries

Country	Currency	ISO Code
Afghanistan	Afghani	AFN
Albania	Albanian lek	ALL
Algeria	Algerian dinar	DZD
Andorra	European euro	EUR
Argentina	Argentine peso	ARS
Armenia	Armenian dram	AMD
Australia	Australian dollar	AUD
Austria	European euro	EUR
Azerbaijan	Azerbaijan manat	AZN
Bahamas	Bahamian dollar	BSD
Bahrain	Bahraini dinar	BHD
Bangladesh	Bangladeshi taka	BDT
Barbados	Barbadian dollar	BBD
Belarus	Belarusian ruble	BYN
Belgium	European euro	EUR
Bolivia	Bolivian boliviano	BOB
Bosnia and Herzegovina	Bosnia and Herzegovina convertible mark	BAM
Brazil	Brazilian real	BRL
Brunei	Brunei dollar	BND
Bulgaria	Bulgarian lev	BGN
Cambodia	Cambodian riel	KHR
Canada	Canadian dollar	CAD
Caribbean Netherlands (Netherlands)	United States dollar	USD
Chile	Chilean peso	CLP

Country	Currency	ISO Code
China	Chinese Yuan Renminbi	CNY
Colombia	Colombian peso	COP
Congo, Democratic Republic of the	Congolese franc	CDF
Costa Rica	Costa Rican colon	CRC
Croatia	Croatian kuna	HRK
Cuba	Cuban peso	CUP
Cyprus	European euro	EUR
Czechia	Czech koruna	CZK
Denmark	Danish krone	DKK
Dominican Republic	Dominican peso	DOP
Ecuador	United States dollar	USD
Egypt	Egyptian pound	EGP
El Salvador	United States dollar	USD
Equatorial Guinea	Central African CFA franc	XAF
Estonia	European euro	EUR
Ethiopia	Ethiopian birr	ETB
Finland	European euro	EUR
France	European euro	EUR
Germany	European euro	EUR
Greece	European euro	EUR
Greenland (Denmark)	Danish krone	DKK
Guatemala	Guatemalan quetzal	GTQ
Guinea	Guinean franc	GNF
Hong Kong (China)	Hong Kong dollar	HKD
Hungary	Hungarian forint	HUF
Iceland	Icelandic krona	ISK
India	Indian rupee	INR

LIST OF CURRENCIES OF THE MAJOR TRADING COUNTRIES

Country	Currency	ISO Code
Indonesia	Indonesian rupiah	IDR
Iran	Iranian rial	IRR
Iraq	Iraqi dinar	IQD
Ireland	European euro	EUR
Israel	Israeli new shekel	ILS
Italy	European euro	EUR
Jamaica	Jamaican dollar	JMD
Japan	Japanese yen	JPY
Kazakhstan	Kazakhstani tenge	KZT
Kenya	Kenyan shilling	KES
Kyrgyzstan	Kyrgyzstani som	KGS
Latvia	European euro	EUR
Lebanon	Lebanese pound	LBP
Liberia	Liberian dollar	LRD
Libya	Libyan dinar	LYD
Lithuania	European euro	EUR
Luxembourg	European euro	EUR
Madagascar	Malagasy ariary	MGA
Malaysia	Malaysian ringgit	MYR
Malta	European euro	EUR
Mexico	Mexican peso	MXN
Moldova	Moldovan leu	MDL
Monaco	European euro	EUR
Montenegro	European euro	EUR
Morocco	Moroccan dirham	MAD
Nepal	Nepalese rupee	NPR
Netherlands	European euro	EUR
New Zealand	New Zealand dollar	NZD
Nigeria	Nigerian naira	NGN

Country	Currency	ISO Code
North Korea	North Korean won	KPW
North Macedonia	Macedonian denar	MKD
Norway	Norwegian krone	NOK
Pakistan	Pakistani rupee	PKR
Palestine	Israeli new shekel	ILS
Panama	United States dollar	USD
Papua New Guinea	Papua New Guinean kina	PGK
Paraguay	Paraguayan guarani	PYG
Peru	Peruvian sol	PEN
Philippines	Philippine peso	PHP
Poland	Polish zloty	PLN
Portugal	European euro	EUR
Puerto Rico (USA)	United States dollar	USD
Qatar	Qatari riyal	QAR
Romania	Romanian leu	RON
Russia	Russian ruble	RUB
Saudi Arabia	Saudi Arabian riyal	SAR
Senegal	West African CFA franc	XOF
Serbia	Serbian dinar	RSD
Singapore	Singapore dollar	SGD
Slovakia	European euro	EUR
Slovenia	European euro	EUR
South Africa	South African rand	ZAR
South Korea	South Korean won	KRW
Spain	European euro	EUR
Sudan	Sudanese pound	SDG
Sweden	Swedish krona	SEK
Switzerland	Swiss franc	CHF
Syria	Syrian pound	SYP

Country	Currency	ISO Code
Taiwan	New Taiwan dollar	TWD
Tanzania	Tanzanian shilling	TZS
Thailand	Thai baht	THB
Tunisia	Tunisian dinar	TND
Turkey	Turkish lira	TRY
Turkmenistan	Turkmen manat	TMT
Ukraine	Ukrainian hryvnia	UAH
United Arab Emirates	UAE dirham	AED
United Kingdom	Pound sterling	GBP
United States of America	United States dollar	USD
Uruguay	Uruguayan peso	UYU
Uzbekistan	Uzbekistani som	UZS
Vatican City (Holy See)	European euro	EUR
Venezuela	Venezuelan bolivar	VES
Vietnam	Vietnamese dong	VND